Excel

YEARS 9 to 10

Reading and Vocabulary Workbook

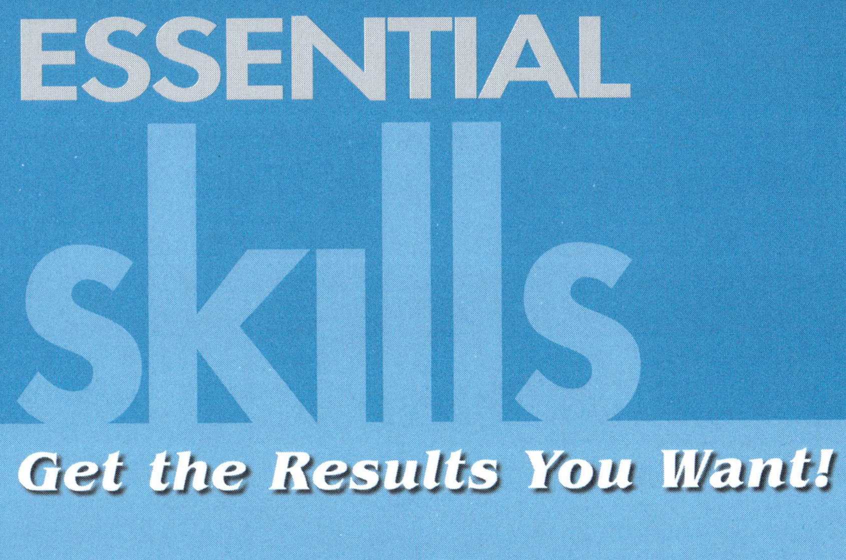

Get the Results You Want!

Maya Puiu

Reprinted 2019, 2022

Reviewed in 2024 for the NSW Curriculum and Australian Curriculum Version 9.0 changes

ISBN 978 1 74125 413 6

Pascal Press
PO Box 250
Glebe NSW 2037
(02) 9198 1748
www.pascalpress.com.au

Publisher: Vivienne Joannou
Project editors: Mark Dixon and Leanne Poll
Edited by Leanne Howard
Series developer and consultant: Kristine Brown
Reviewed by Justine Hodgson
Cover and page design by DiZign Pty Ltd
Typeset by lj Design (Julianne Billington)
Images by dreamstime.com
Printed by Vivar Printing/Green Giant Press

Contents

To the student

This book is designed to lead you through some essential reading skills as well as develop your vocabulary and language. Reading more, and thinking and writing about what you are reading, will develop your skills as an English student. First you will strengthen your reading comprehension skills; then you will develop your understanding of the language and literary techniques that writers use to achieve a particular purpose for a particular audience.

Each unit is divided into six sections. The exercises and examples in each unit relate as much as possible to the main reading text used.

Before you read—*this section contains pre-reading activities designed to get you thinking about the text you are about to read and engage with.*

Test your understanding—*this section contains a range of comprehension questions that will test your understanding of the text you have just read.*

Boost your reading skills—*this section will focus on a particular reading skill, such as understanding main ideas and deducing the meaning of words.*

Work on words—*this section focuses on improving your vocabulary and understanding of words.*

Spotlight on language—*this section focuses you on an aspect of language that is present in each unit.*

Extend your skills—*this last question allows you to extend and develop the ideas presented in the unit.*

Take your time when completing the exercises and think carefully about what skill each exercise is trying to teach you. This book will help you become a better reader and give you skills that you can use when reading new and different texts.

I wish you the best of luck and I hope you enjoy the activities.

Maya Puiu

UNIT ONE

SBS Reporters' Blog

Before you read

The questions in this section help you focus on your **background knowledge** and **prior experiences** of the topic. Activating this background knowledge helps you make **connections** between new and known information.

1 Were you, or any members of your family, born overseas?

2 What do you think it means to be Australian?

3 Do you think that what it means to be Australian has changed over time; for example, since when your parents were young?

SBS Reporters' Blog

http://www.sbsworldnews.com

Reporter's Blog

1 Thirty-one years ago today I was born to a wonderful Portuguese immigrant family in a hospital in Wollongong on the South Coast of New South Wales, with a full birth name of Ricardo Jorge Goncalves (Jorge, pronounced George, not hor-hay).

But, despite the very, very Portuguese name, I'm as Aussie as they come.

As we approach Australia Day, it got me wondering what being Australian really means. What is the Australian culture? What does a typical Australian look like these days? Is Australia truly multicultural?

Last night, in his Australia Day address, neurosurgeon Dr Charlie Teo spoke of the racism he endured and, more recently, his daughter, despite their obvious Australian accents. They have Asian backgrounds.

2 Growing up in Wollongong I spent the first five years of my life speaking Portuguese as my first language. It wasn't really until I hit primary school when English was really introduced, and it was in my first year , when the nuns anointed me "Richard".

3 Neither I nor my family really questioned it or made a big deal about it. It kind of just happened. Instead of being called Ricardo at school, I was Richard. The bizarre thing was that I probably went to one of the most ethnically diverse Catholic primary schools in Wollongong, so surely it wasn't because of my cultural background or an attempt to anglicise me.

4 So, throughout my schooling life I was Richard Goncalves (Gone-karlves). I excelled at school, even topping my English classes culminating in 3 unit English at high school (I never want to hear about Utopias and Anti-Utopias again) and was the College Captain at my high school, Edmund Rice College. At the same time I worked hard to earn a bit of cash, respected my family and contributed to the local Portuguese community dancing at my local folk group and the Wollongong community at large through various endeavours.

5 I was your typical Aussie kid growing up, I just happened to have a Portuguese family who worked tremendously hard and ate lots of espetada and on the odd occasion, milho. Look them up.

Did I ever feel a sense of racism directly aimed at me? Not really, but in my early adulthood, I was told by a nightclub bouncer in Wollongong that I was refused entry into a club because my hair was too dark. It was a common excuse.

6 Richard stuck with me for 24 years, even as I started work on air as a journalist. Again, I didn't question it and I didn't think much about it to be honest. My birth certificate and official documents said Ricardo, everything else, Richard. Even my parents were calling me Richard.

7 But when given the chance to work at SBS, it was suggested that maybe I'd like to return to my birth name. What a great opportunity to really help define what it is to be Australian.

So I have a woggy name. It's actually not that woggy. But hey, that's who I am, and that's what it is to be Australian. (And a chance to get some publicity and attention for myself for the name change. I do have a marketing degree after all.)

8 Australia is a melting pot of different nationalities, respecting each other to help live the Australian way. What is the Australian way? Ignore the stereotypes it's not about throwing a shrimp on the BBQ or slapping Vegemite on some burnt toast.

Nor, to the other extent is it about cultural exclusion.

9 It's about people that live in Australia who come from different backgrounds simply respect each other, to help each other strive to be the best they can be and the best this young country can be.

It's as simple as that.

10 I'm Ricardo Goncalves, I'm Australian, I just happen to have a Portuguese background. It doesn't define me. What does is the way I treat and respect my fellow Aussies.

Oh, and it's my birthday today, two days before Australia Day. That's pretty Aussie hey?

Your Comments

25 Jan 2012 21:48 AEST
asianaustralian
From: sydney

lovely reading

thanks for your thoughts, love to read stuff like this. so that i shouldn't have define myself as 'asianaustralian'!! all the more power to the likes of you (us). i love having you as my hero & role model <3

Agree (3 people agree) **Disagree** (0 people disagree)

---

24 Jan 2012 18:42 AEST
Sean
From: St Marys, sydney

Happy Birthday!

Great post. As far as stereotypes go, we're all immigrants, unless you're a full blood Aboriginal. As far as I'm concerned, if you live here, you're an aussie. Simple as that. Celebrate it in whatever way takes your fancy, as long as it doesn't get ugly for others. That's REALLY 'un-australian'. And happy Australia day to all at SBS, whether we see/hear you or not you're all a bunch of champions in my book.

Agree (10 people agree) **Disagree** (0 people disagree)

Test your understanding

1 Tick (✓) the correct answer. Who is Ricardo Goncalves?

a a blog commenter ______
b a Portuguese immigrant ______
c an SBS television presenter ______
d a neurosurgeon ______

2 Tick (✓) the correct answer. Which answer best describes this reporter's blog?

a an inside look at the experiences of a television presenter ______
b a news report ______
c an opportunity for the public to comment on current affairs ______
d a profile and summary of an SBS reporter ______

3 Tick (✓) the correct answer. Blogs can be classified by their topic or subject, also known as genre. Which genre does this blog fit into?

a political opinion ______
b music and the arts ______
c social commentary ______
d the environment ______

4 Tick (✓) the correct answer. What is the purpose of Ricardo Goncalves' blog?

a to present information about his Portuguese ancestry ______
b to explain why he has changed his name ______
c to discuss what it means to be Australian ______
d to share his experiences of racism as a teenager ______

5 Look back at the text and underline the best definition of the following words. You should use the context of the sentence to help you work out the meaning.

a *ethnically diverse* (paragraph 3):	culturally individual	culturally varied	culturally similar
b *anglicise* (paragraph 3):	make english	make religious	make diverse
c *culminating in* (paragraph 4):	adding in	resulting in	mixing in
d *melting pot* (paragraph 8):	mixture	environment	process
e *stereotype* (paragraph 8):	a fixture	a barrier	a fixed idea

6 Tick (✓) the correct answer. In paragraph 2, Ricardo tells you that the nuns *anointed* him Richard. What does *anointed* mean in this sentence?

a daubed ______
b christened ______
c named ______
d offered ______

7 Tick (✓) the correct answer. In paragraph 8, Ricardo tells you that to him, being Australian is not about *cultural exclusion*. What does *cultural exclusion* mean?

- **a** being accepting of different cultures ______
- **b** rejecting people based on perceived cultural differences ______
- **c** government regulations about who can immigrate to Australia ______
- **d** allowing residents to decide who may enter Australia, and who may not ______

8 Tick (✓) the correct answer. In paragraph 9, when Ricardo says 'It's as simple as that', what is he referring to?

- **a** what it really means to live as an Australian ______
- **b** assisting Australia to go forward as a young country ______
- **c** his own experiences as a Portuguese-Australian ______
- **d** allowing people from different backgrounds to live in Australia ______

9 Use your own words to explain what you believe is the overall message of the article.

____

____

____

____

____

Boost your reading skills

Reading and recognising informal style

A blogger is someone who blogs or writes content for a **blog**. A blog is like an online journal or diary, although it can also be used for online journalism. As a result, a blog's language is informal and personal. People who respond to a blog's contents by writing a comment also use features of informal language.

Informal language is similar to a spoken conversation. Informal language may include:

- **slang** (e.g. *chick*—a female; *slack*—lazy; *gross*—something unpleasant)
- **figures of speech** (e.g. alliteration, hyperbole, idiom, oxymoron, pun or simile)
- **asides**—this is where we add extra information. When written, an aside may be enclosed in brackets (like this) or dashes (—). Sometimes asides may not have brackets or dashes to indicate them (e.g. when Ricardo says 'Look them up')
- **colloquial language**, which is common everyday language (e.g. *g'day, I wanna* or *I'm gonna*).

1 Look at the reporter's blog again and locate examples of the following **informal language**.

- **a** colloquial language ______________________________
- **b** an aside ______________________________
- **c** a figure of speech ______________________________

Informal writing adopts a personal tone as if you were speaking directly to the reader. You can use the first-person point of view (*I* and *we*), and you are likely to address the reader using the second person (*you* and *your*). Ricardo sometimes uses short informal sentences that contain no pronouns, but that work in the same way.

For example: In paragraph 5 he says 'Look them up' but what he really means is '*You* should look them up'. This adds to the conversational style of the text.

2 Find an example from the reporter's blog where Ricardo Goncalves uses the **first person** *I* and *we* and uses the second person *you* or *your*.

a *I* ____________________

b *we* ____________________

c *you/your* ____________________

3 What do you think is the effect of these pronouns on the reader?

a *I* ____________________

b *we* ____________________

c *you/your* ____________________

Other features of informal written texts include:

- short sentences—these are sometimes essential to making a point in informal writing
- words that are likely to be simplified using contractions (e.g. *I'm*, *doesn't*, *couldn't* or *it's*) and abbreviations (e.g. *TV*, *photos*) whenever possible
- feelings—the author might invite the reader to appreciate and share their experiences.

4 Rewrite the following excerpt from the reporter's blog by changing the language from **informal** to **formal**.

You can do this by:

- **making conversational language more formal** (e.g. *a big deal* → commotion/controversy)
- **removing the contractions** (e.g. *can't*) by writing the word in full (e.g. *cannot*)
- **removing personalised language** by eliminating personal pronouns (*I*, *we* or *you*)
- **using the third-person** perspective instead (e.g. *Ricardo* instead of *I*).

Neither I nor my family really questioned it or made a big deal about it. It kind of just happened. Instead of being called Ricardo at school, I was Richard. The bizarre thing was that I probably went to one of the most ethnically diverse Catholic primary schools in Wollongong, so surely it wasn't because of my cultural background or an attempt to anglicise me.

Work on words

Clichés

Clichés are **metaphors** and **expressions** that have become tired through overuse. *Better late than never* is a cliché, as is *hungry as a horse* and *cried over spilt milk*. It is not just old expressions that can become clichéd—think of examples like *at the end of the day*, *absolutely* and *a big deal*. In literature, clichés are words and phrases, once interesting, which have lost their original effect from overuse. However, clichés are used commonly by speakers in **conversation** and **informal texts** and are a common feature of everyday language.

We use clichés without thinking, sometimes because they *fit the bill* or *hit the nail on the head* (both clichés), but usually because they're **metaphors** or **idioms** that have become so common that we no longer notice them. We often use these expressions when we speak or write to make our meaning **clear** and **accessible** to the person we are communicating with.

1 Test your recognition of the following common **clichés** by filling in the missing words.

a Busy as a ____________________.

b On a wild ____________________ chase.

c The early bird catches the ____________________.

d ____________________ things come to those who wait.

e A penny ____________________ is a penny earned.

f An ____________________ a day keeps the doctor away.

g Don't put all your ____________________ in one basket.

h Wake up and smell the ____________________.

i Better late than ____________________.

j Raining ____________________ and ____________________.

Clichés are a feature of the reporter's blog as they contribute to the **informal** and **conversational tone** of the text. However, when you are writing other texts it is important to read through your article or story with a critical eye and to not be afraid to revise and change your ideas.

2 Look at the following excerpts from the reporters' blog. Clichéd words and ideas have been underlined. Rewrite each sentence so that the ideas become more original and **less clichéd**.

a Australia is a <u>melting pot</u> of different nationalities.

____

____

b I'm as <u>Aussie as they come</u>.

____

____

c Richard stuck with me for 24 years.

d It's as simple as that.

e When he hit primary school, the nuns made him 'Richard'.

f Neither I nor my family really questioned it or made a big deal about it.

Spotlight on language

Blog comments

A **blog** is a web-based publication made up of entries and **comments**, or 'posts'. Blog comments allow readers to voice their **opinions** and **ideas** on the subject being discussed. All posts appear in reverse chronological order so that the most recent entry appears first. A blog is a **public document** that encourages a community approach to writing and sharing ideas.

While many blogs you encounter may appear rushed and contain spelling errors, there is no reason why the blogs you write shouldn't be written properly, using **correct grammar** and have a **clear** and **logical structure**. In this way, your opinions will be presented intelligently and will make a meaningful contribution to the community discussion.

Blog writing guidelines

- Capitalise letters at the beginning of sentences and proper nouns (names of people and places).
- Write using complete sentences.
- Use correct punctuation.
- Use correct spelling.
- Don't repeat yourself.

1 **a** Find the errors and rewrite the blog **comment**. There are two capital letters missing, and there is one repetition and one spelling error.

24 Jan 2012 18:42 AEST
Sean
From: St Marys, sydney

Happy Birthday!

Great post. As far as stereotypes go, we're all immigrants, unless you're a full blood Aboriginal. As far as I'm concerned, if you live here, you're an aussie. Simple as that. Celebrate it in whatever way takes your fancy, as long as it doesn't get ugly for others. That's REALLY 'un-australian'. And happy Australia day to all at SBS, whether we see/hear you or not you're all a bunch of champions in my book.

Agree (10 people agree) **Disagree** (0 people disagree)

b Find the errors and rewrite the blog **comment**. There are seven capital letters missing and there is one full stop and one *I* missing. One full stop should be a comma and there should be one apostrophe.

25 Jan 2012 21:48 AEST
asianaustralian
From: sydney

lovely reading

thanks for your thoughts, love to read stuff like this. so that i shouldn't have define myself as 'asianaustralian'!! all the more power to the likes of you (us). i love having you as my hero & role model <3

Agree (3 people agree) **Disagree** (0 people disagree)

Make **high-level vocabulary** choices—don't always choose the simplest word you can think of as you want to contribute intelligent and thoughtful ideas.

2 Here are some common words that are quite simple. Find similar words (**synonyms**) that are bigger, more descriptive and higher-level vocabulary choices. The first one has been done for you.

a happy joyful, cheerful, blissful, exalted

b sad __________

c bad __________

d angry __________

e small __________

f big __________

Give a **compliment**—even though you may not agree with all ideas in the article you are responding to, you should be able to find a few ideas that you agree with or appreciate. Giving a compliment to the writer of the article is a way to contribute to the discussion in a positive and non-aggressive manner.

3 Find two **ideas** from the SBS reporters' blog that you enjoyed or agreed with.

a I particularly liked your idea about __________

b I would like to compliment you on your blog. It made me feel __________ when you mentioned __________

Ask a **question**—asking a question can help you add to the discussion rather than just repeating ideas. Other people writing blog comments may answer your questions and sometimes the writer of the article will respond to your question in a blog comment as well.

4 Write two questions that you would like to ask Ricardo Goncalves about his **blog post**.

a __________

b __________

Extend your skills

What is your **opinion** on this topic?

Bring together all your **ideas** and write your own **blog comment** in response to the SBS reporters' blog. Make sure your spelling and grammar are correct, make **high-level vocabulary** choices and include one **compliment** and one **question**.

UNIT TWO

Q&A

Before you read

Making predictions is more than just guessing what is going to happen next. Predicting helps you become **actively involved** while you read a text and helps you remember information for longer.

Read only the first THREE questions of the text below and then answer the following questions.

1 Has Alice Pung written the stories in *Growing up Asian in Australia*? How do you know this?

---

2 The group responsible for the text below is *Black Inc. Books*. Who do you think they might be?

---

3 *Q&A* stands for 'questions and answers' and is similar to an interview. What do you think will be the purpose of the *Q&A* below?

Growing up Asian in Australia—Q&A with Alice Pung

1. *What made you want to edit a collection of stories and essays about growing up Asian in Australia?*

My editors at Black Inc. and I got together one day and brainstormed this idea, because although Asian-Australians had been in Australia since around 1810, there was such a dearth of stories about their experiences and contributions to this country.

2. *How did you go about selecting which pieces to include?*

I concentrated on the period of 'growing up'—because that's the period when must of life's 'firsts' happen—and I also wanted the definition of Asian-Australian to be as diverse and inclusive as possible. I selected pieces that reflected a broad range of Asian-Australian experience, so we have stories ranging from Jenny Kee's adolescent awakening, to Tony Ayres' account of blowing a kiss to a racist skinhead, from Tanveer Ahmed's hilarious meditation on the exotic rissole to Shalini Althil's attempts to be the first ethnically-enhanced Wonder Woman, from Khoa Do's mentoring of young disadvantaged Australians, to the experiences of the first Asian presenter of Play School—and everything in between. We have writers like Kylie Kwong and Ken Chau whose ancestors came from the gold rush days in the 1860s and lived through the White Australia Policy, and more recent arrivals who grew up during the era of multiculturalism. We have writers who are Eurasian, adopted, and migrants. I wanted this anthology to encompass as much diverse insight as possible, so our authors come from every walk of life.

3. *Were you surprised by the amount of interest you received in the project after calling for submissions?*

I was very happy about the incredible amount of interest received after calling for submissions. Our younger contributors have a wonderful freshness of voice, but we were also especially honoured to receive stories from Asian-Australians from older generations, because they could reflect back on their growing-up years with the wisdom of experience. We also have quite a few stories about how different generations dealt with their parents, and I only wish I had this amount of insight when I was growing up! I also wish there was more room in the anthology to include many more of the stories we received. It was such an honour to read them all.

4. Are there common themes running through the collection? Do the contributors share a common experience of growing up?

The pieces in this anthology—like Asian-Australians—are so diverse, and the beauty of this book is that it shatters all stereotypes people may have had about Asian-Australians—we have eminent Asian-Australians like Lord Mayor So revealing that he came to Australia to follow in the footsteps of Chinese-American Nobel Physics Prize-winners, stories about Asian-Australians surviving different types of racist bullying throughout the decades and stories of Asian-Australians 'coming out' to their parents. What moved me was the resilience of our writers, their creativity, humour, quirk and insight—sometimes against severe racism, personal illness, familial pressure and pressure from society to conform.

5. Given that this book is all about growing up Asian, would you recommend it to a nan-Asian reader?

Although this collection is titled *Growing up Asian in Australia*, I wanted to bring out the common humanity of our authors, so that any reader could pick up the book and be amused, amazed, moved and heartened. There is often the stereotype of Asian-Australians as the 'model minority' (and before that, we were considered the Yellow Peril). What this anthology aims to do is dismantle all these stereotypes and show the incredible diversity of experience of our lives, the humour and insigh, the struggles and achievements—these stories should be very much part of the Australian narrative, because they are also very Australian stories.

From *Growing Up Asian in Australia*, edited by Alice Pung (Black Inc. Books, 2008)

Test your understanding

1 Tick (✓) the correct answer. Who is Alice Pung?

- **a** an interviewer ______
- **b** a memoir writer ______
- **c** an editor at *Black Inc. Books* ______
- **d** the editor of *Growing Up Asian in Australia* ______

2 Tick (✓) the correct answer. *Growing up Asian in Australia* is an example of a non-fiction text. This term could be applied to many types of texts but based on what you have read in the Q&A, what does it mean here?

- **a** a story about different people's lives and experiences ______
- **b** something that could appear in an encyclopedia ______
- **c** dealing with real events and people and based on truth ______
- **d** a report on a situation including facts and statistics ______

3 Tick (✓) the correct answer. Find the word 'dearth' in the Q&A. Use the context of the sentence it appears in to find its best definition.

- **a** demise ______
- **b** departure ______
- **c** deficiency ______
- **d** withdrawal ______

4 In the Q&A paragraph 2, Pung wants the definition of 'Asian-Australian' to be as 'diverse and inclusive' as possible. What does she mean by this?

______

______

______

5 In the Q&A paragraph 2, Pung provides a few examples of the types of experiences recorded in her book. Which one do you find the most interesting and why?

____

____

____

____

6 Tick (✓) the correct answer. The book 'shatters all stereotypes' people may have about Asian-Australians (Q&A paragraph 4). What does this mean?

a It exposes generalisations people have made about Asian personality types. ______

b It turns people's expectations of how Asians live and behave upside down. ______

c It encourages and maintains generalisations about Asians. ______

d It creates an angry response to negative stereotyping of Asian-Australians. ______

7 Tick (✓) the correct answer. In the Q&A paragraph 4, what are said to be the 'common themes' that run through the collection?

a bullying ______

b revealing the 'truth' about Asian-Australian experiences ______

c creativity, quirk and insight ______

d there are no common themes as each story is unique and diverse ______

8 Pung provides many examples of the different types of writers and offers a diverse range of their experiences. Why does she do this?

____

____

____

____

____

____

____

9 What do you think 'Tanveer Ahmed's hilarious meditation on the exotic rissole' will be about? (Q&A paragraph 2)

a a humorous thought and reflection on multicultural food in Australia

b Buddhist attitudes towards meat eaters and promotion of vegetarianism

c a funny anecdote about meditation and mysterious food

d Australian experiences of Asian cooking experiences

10 Read the Q&A paragraph 5 again. Underline the best summary of ideas from the following list.

- **a** The anthology aims to focus on what makes us all human.
- **b** The anthology aims to tell Australian stories about Australians.
- **c** The anthology is designed for anyone to read, at any time.

11 'There is often the stereotype of Asian-Australians as the model minority' (paragraph 5). A minority is a smaller number of a whole, meaning that Asian-Australians make up only a small percentage of the entire Australian population. Which statement best describes what it means to be a 'model minority'?

- **a** A model minority is a small group that contains ideal and desirable personality traits.
- **b** A model minority is a small group that exhibits undesirable behaviour.
- **c** A model minority is a small group that creates diversity in Australian society.
- **d** A model minority is a small group that is also known as the 'Yellow Peril'.

Boost your reading skills

Understanding complex sentences

Skilful writers use a variety of sentences to make their writing **interesting** and **dynamic**. Too many simple sentences, for example, make writing basic and immature while too many long and complex sentences make writing complicated, dense and hard to understand. When reading, you sometimes need to work hard to determine the **main message** in long and complex sentences. The main message is contained in the **main** or **independent clause**.

Quickly revise your understanding of sentence types by studying the following explanations.

- **Simple sentence**—a simple sentence, also called an **independent clause**, contains a subject and a verb, and expresses a complete thought. It is a sentence that 'stands alone' and makes sense by itself.

  For example: Growing up is hard.

- **Compound sentence**—a compound sentence contains two **independent clauses** joined by a **conjunction** (a joining word), such as *for*, *and*, *nor*, *but*, *or*, *yet* or *so*. Except for very short sentences, you should always use a comma before a conjunction.

  For example: Growing up is hard, **yet** it is also fun (the independent clauses are underlined and the conjunction **highlighted**).

- **Complex sentence**—a complex sentence has an **independent clause** joined by one or more dependent clauses. A **dependent clause** is a sentence that 'depends' on another, and cannot 'stand alone'. A dependent clause always contains words such as *because*, *since*, *after*, *although*, *when*, *that*, *who* or *which*.

  For example: **Although growing up is hard**, it is also fun (the independent clause is underlined and the dependent clause is **highlighted**).

- **Compound-complex**—a compound-complex sentence contains a mixture of independent clauses and dependent clauses, with **at least one compound sentence**.

  For example: **Although growing up is hard** (dependent clause), it is also fun (independent clause), and can be full of exciting and enjoyable experiences (independent clause).

1 In the following examples, underline the **independent clauses** and circle the **dependent clause** (it will contain *because, since, after, although,* or *when*, or a relative pronoun such as *that, who,* or *which*). The first one has been done for you.

a After she had grown up, she realised how precious childhood really was.

b Although it rained a lot we still spent hours at the beach when we were kids.

c We loved to go away in the car during school holidays.

d After school I hope to continue study at university.

e He felt much better after realising other people felt the same way.

f The people who I grew up with are still my friends.

2 One of the main strategies in understanding complex sentences is finding the main independent clause. Underline the **main independent clause** in each of the following examples from the Q&A. You might only find one independent clause or you might find more than one.

a Although this collection is titled *Growing up Asian in Australia*, I wanted to bring out the common humanity of our authors, so that any reader could pick up the book and be amused, amazed, moved and heartened.

b I concentrated on the period of 'growing up'—because that's the period when most of life's 'firsts' happen—and I also wanted the definition on Asian Australian to be as diverse and inclusive as possible.

c I was very happy about the incredible amount of interest received after calling for submissions.

d We also have quite a few stories about how different generations dealt with their parents and I only wish I had this amount of insight when I was growing up!

e Our younger contributors have a wonderful freshness of voice, but we were also especially honoured to receive stories from Asian-Australians from older generations, because they could reflect back on their growing-up years with the wisdom of experience.

f I wanted this anthology to encompass as much diverse insight as possible, so our authors come from every walk of life.

Work on words

Troublesome words

English contains many examples of **troublesome words** that can be confusing when reading and writing.

Troublesome words might include:

* **words that sound the same as another word but are spelt differently**, also known as homophones (e.g. *current* and *currant*)
* **words that are similar in sound and spelling to another word** and as a result are often confused (e.g. *precede* and *proceed*).

In the following example from the *Growing Up Asian in Australia Q&A*, the word *dearth* means 'shortage' or 'scarcity'. However, if read quickly you may have thought this read 'death', which changes the meaning of the sentence.

For example: ... because although Asian-Australians had been in this country since around 1810, there was such a **dearth** of stories about their experiences and contributions to this country.

1 Underline the correct **troublesome word** in the following sentences. The first one has been done for you.

- **a** The apartment was (leased/least) to the travellers for the summer season.
- **b** The (least/leased) the hotel can do is apologise for the inconvenience they caused.
- **c** The student used to (pour/pore) ______________ over his books all night before an exam.
- **d** I like to keep in touch with (current/currant) ______________ affairs so I know what's going on in the world.
- **e** My grandmother would pop a (current/currant) ______________ on the top of each delicious scone.
- **f** The employee indicated that we should (proceed/precede) ______________ towards the counter.
- **g** The school principal should (proceed/precede) ______________ other staff when she enters the hall.
- **h** I am not usually (adverse/averse) ______________ to a hot cup of coffee in the mornings.
- **i** There are usually (adverse/averse) ______________ effects to drinking and driving.

Now try to create your own sentences using the following pairs of **troublesome words**. You may need to use a dictionary to help you.

2 adapt/adept

- **a** ____
- **b** ____

3 ensure/insure

- **a** ____
- **b** ____

4 compliment/complement

- **a** ____
- **b** ____

5 effect/affect

- **a** ____
- **b** ____

Spotlight on language

Personal language

Writers use **personal language** to communicate ideas about their thoughts, experiences and opinions.

These language features are typical of personal texts:

- **first-person** perspective (*I, me, mine*)
- **directly addressing** the reader (*you*)
- **rhetorical questions** to the reader (e.g. How would ***you*** have felt?)
- referring to own **thought processes** and **feelings** (e.g. as **I** reflected on **my** actions later)
- using **adjectives**, **adverbs** and **descriptive verbs** which express attitudes and opinions (e.g. *anxious, timidly, fascinate*).

1 Look at the following examples of personal language from the book *Growing up Asian in Australia.* Underline words you think contribute to the **personal tone** of the sentence. The first one has been done for you.

a I admired his crew cut and was riveted by his rat's tail, which he sported with great confidence. I wished I had a rat's tail, but my parents were horrified.

b It was embarrassing to be good at studies and I tried to hide my scholastic abilities as much as possible.

c I'd watch them intently: like an outsider, like a tourist

d My attempts to blend in failed as soon as I opened my mouth.

e Now that I thought about it, everything up to that point in my life seemed so incredibly abnormal compared to everyone else I knew.

f To this day I am to some extent confused … am I more Asian or Australian?

g If I couldn't express myself, who was myself?

2 Now look at the following statements that contain factual and objective language. Re-write each one using **personal language**. The first one has been done for you.

a Most teenagers use social media as a way of communicating with their peers.

I couldn't live without the internet or Facebook! How would I keep in touch with everyone?

b The top wish among all teen girls is for their parents to communicate better with them. This includes frequent and more open conversations.

c Changing brains mean that adolescents act differently from adults.

d Adolescents are more likely to act on impulse.

e Healthy eating in childhood and adolescence is important for proper growth and development and can prevent health problems.

Extend your skills

1 What other books have you read and liked about growing up, or about growing up as part of a minority group of some kind? Provide the title and author, include if it was fiction or non-fiction and write a sentence explaining what the book was about.

2 Imagine you are continuing the Q&A. What are two more questions you could ask author Alice Pung about her memoir collection, *Growing up Asian in Australia*?

a

b

UNIT THREE

Wikipedia page

Before you read

It is always easier to understand what you are reading if you have some **background knowledge** and **experience** of the text type and mode of communication.

1 What do you know about Wikipedia—who creates the information? Is it considered reliable?

2 How often do you use Wikipedia when searching the net for information? Do you use any other website regularly when locating information?

3 In general, what type of information do you use Wikipedia to locate? Do you use it for school assignments or to satisfy your own curiosity? Do you use it for particular subjects or for looking up information about celebrities, music or movies?

Wikipedia page for *Oodgeroo Noonuccal*

Oodgeroo Noonuccal

1 **Oodgeroo Noonuccal** (/ˈʊdˌɡəˌruː/ /ˈnuːˌnəˌkəl/ *Uud-gə-ruu nuu-nə-kal*;) born **Kathleen Jean Mary Ruska**, formerly **Kath Walker**) (3 November 1920–16 September 1993) was an Australian poet, political activist, artist and educator. She was also a campaigner for Aboriginal rights. Oodgeroo was best known for her poetry, and was the first Aboriginal Australian to publish a book of verse.

Birth and early life

2 Noonuccal was the second youngest of six children to parents Ted and Lucy Ruska. Ted was a labourer and led a strike in 1935; he instilled a fierce sense of justice in his daughter, with whom he shared the dreaming totem Kabul (the carpet snake). She wrote the poems *Municipal Gum* and *Understand Old One*.

3 Noonuccal loved the sea and the seashore, but not her schooling. She wrote with her left hand, and was punished for it. She left school at age 13 in 1933, in the depths of the Depression, to work as a

domestic servant in Brisbane. In 1942, during World War II with her brothers Eddie and Eric imprisoned as POWs in Singapore, she volunteered for war service in the Australian Women's Army Service. As a communication worker in Army HQ in Brisbane she received training in book keeping, typing and shorthand, reaching the rank of corporal. During her war service "Oodgeroo noticed a big difference in the way she was treated once she had enlisted. She experienced social equality."

Life as a poet and activist

4 As she lived through the 1960s she began to emerge as a prominent figure, both as a political activist and as a writer. She was Queensland state secretary of the Federal Council for the Advancement of Aboriginal and Torres Strait Islanders (FCAATSI), and was involved in a number of other political organisations. She was a key figure in the campaign for the reform of the Australian constitution to allow Aboriginal people full citizenship, lobbying Prime Minister Robert Menzies in 1965, and his successor Harold Holt in 1966. At one deputation in 1963, she taught Robert Menzies a lesson in the realities of Aboriginal life. After offering the deputation an alcoholic drink, he was startled to learn that in Queensland he could be jailed for doing the same thing.

5 She wrote many books, beginning with *We Are Going* (1964), the first book to be published by an Aboriginal woman. The title poem concludes:

The scrubs are gone, the hunting and the laughter.
The eagle is gone, the emu and the kangaroo are gone from this place.
The bora ring is gone.
The corroboree is gone.
And we are going.

Adapted from http://en.wikipedia.org/wiki/Oodgeroo_Noonuccal

Test your understanding

1 Tick (✓) the correct answer. What name is Oodgeroo Noonuccal best known by?

a Kath Walker ______

b Kathleen Jean Mary Ruska ______

c Oodgeroo Noonuccal ______

d Oodgeroo ______

2 The article does not tell you, but can you guess why she is known by a variety of names?

____

3 Tick (✓) the correct answer. After Oodgeroo's name some unusual text appears: /ˈʊdˌɡəˌruː/ /ˈnuːˌnəˌkəl/. What is this text?

a Aboriginal language ______

b information that helps you pronounce her name ______

c a link to more information about Oodgeroo Noonuccal ______

d a link to a dictionary definition ______

4 Tick (✓) the correct answer. Oodgeroo's father instilled in her 'a fiery sense of justice'. Why would he do this?

a he was a political activist ______

b he was honest ______

c he was angry ______

d he wanted his daughter to be like him ______

5 Tick (✓) the correct answer. What is the text written in blue known as?

a a definition ______

b italics ______

c a hyperlink ______

d a wiki link ______

6 Tick (✓) the correct answer. Using what you know about Aboriginal culture and re-reading paragraph 4, which word below could best replace the word *totem* in that paragraph?

a symbol ______

b support ______

c relationship ______

d sculpture ______

7 Tick (✓) the correct answer. Which of the following statements best captures Oodgeroo's school experience?

a She enjoyed school but had to leave early to get a job. ______

b She enjoyed school except for not being permitted to write with her left hand. ______

c She did not enjoy school because she was not permitted to write with her left hand. ______

d She did not enjoy her time at school and preferred being by the seaside. ______

8 During her war service 'Oodgeroo noticed a big difference in the way she was treated once she had enlisted. She experienced social equality.' In your own words, explain what you think this means.

____

____

____

____

____

Boost your reading skills

Effective web searching

You will often need to **research** information on the internet for school projects and assignments. There are more than 11.5 billion web pages publicly available on the web so locating relevant and valid information can be a complex task. Understanding effective ways to search for information will help you narrow your search and locate information more effectively.

When **searching** on the **web** it is useful to ask yourself about what precisely you need to know—what search terms will produce the most useful results? Effective searchers do not type full questions into search tools.

1 Why do you think it might be ineffective to type a full question into a search engine?

You need to take a question or research topic and transform it into an **effective search term**.

There are three main strategies you can use:

- **identify key words**—these are words that are essential to communicating your need. Key words are often common or proper nouns, but they can also be other words.
- **identify 'maybe' words**—these are words that you don't know if you need or not. There might be different ways of expressing the same idea or there might be ideas that you need to convey, but the words of the question don't seem like the way someone might state the question in writing.
- **ignore unnecessary words**—these are usually little words that add no special meaning to your search and should be left out.

In order to begin a **web search**, you need to first start with a question.

For example: What impact has Oodgeroo Noonuccal had on modern Australia?

Note: the key words are circled and the 'maybe' words are underlined. Unnecessary words are ignored.

Impact is a 'maybe' word as it is a concept that could be expressed in a variety of ways. Identifying synonyms for this word, such as *influence*, *effect* or *impression*, would improve your search terms.

Using a tilde (~) next to your 'maybe' word will search for a word and all its synonyms.

Based on the above process, the search terms would be:

~impact Oodgeroo Noonuccal modern Australia

2 Now write your own question about Oodgeroo Noonuccal. If you wanted to find out more about Oodgeroo Noonuccal after reading her Wikipedia page, what question might you ask?

a What are the **key words** in your question?

b What are the '**maybe**' words?

c Are there any words that need to be **changed** in order to improve the search?

d What are the **unnecessary words**?

e What will your final **search terms** be?

3 Try your search terms out in Google. Look at your results and see if you can find the answer you need, or determine if you need to **revise** your **query** a bit more. Searching is a process and sometimes it might take a few tries to discover the right query. Practise looking at your results and asking yourself, 'What happened? What worked? What didn't?'

How can you further refine your search?

Google provides many tips and shortcuts for internet searching that are extremely useful. They can be found at <http://static.googleusercontent.com/media/www.google.com/en//educators/downloads/Tips_Tricks_17x22.pdf>.

Google also provides a daily search challenge at <www.agoogleaday.com>.

The questions are generally constructed to help practise key-word choice and develop a skill for breaking a larger question into smaller pieces. Why don't you give it a try?

Work on words

Language of information technology

Every interest and occupation has its own special language or **terms**. There's a language for music, crocheting, bookkeeping and football. A **technical term** is a word or phrase that is used in ways that only make sense in that context or situation. You will often find examples of technical language when reading about the internet.

1 The following key concepts and terms are specific to the topic of the internet and Wikipedia. Find the image that best **visually represents** the **concept** of each definition. The first one has been done for you.

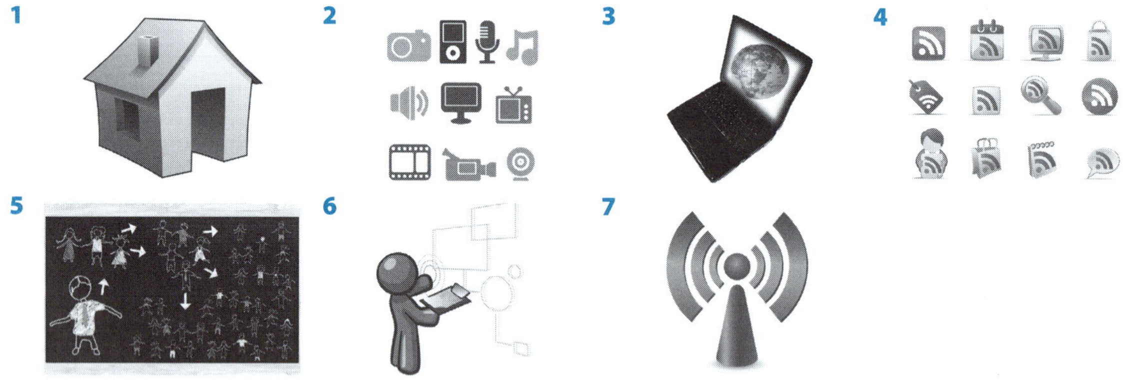

a homepage—this refers to the front page, directory index or main web page of the website of a group, company, organisation or individual. image 1

b links—these allow users to 'jump' to a new web page or a completely different website by clicking on a highlighted and underlined word or phrase on a page. ____________

c podcast—a series of audio or video digital media files which is distributed over the internet. ____________

d RSS—a family of web feed formats used to publish frequently updated works such as blog entries, news headlines, audio and video in a standardised format. ____________

e wiki—software that allows users to create and edit web page content using any web browser. ____________

f World Wide Web—a global information system on the internet which allows documents to be connected to other documents by hypertext links, enabling the user to search for information by moving from one document to another. ____________

g multimedia—the use of a variety of artistic or communicative media. The additional incorporation of sound and/or video can effectively increase engagement with the topic. ____________

2 Could you create a more effective symbol or image to represent the **terms** above? Choose two to focus on and record them here. Briefly annotate each in order to explain your choice.

a **Term:** ____________

Description: ____________

____

____

b **Term:** ____________

Description: ____________

____

____

Spotlight on language

Wiki principles

Wikipedia is an online encyclopedia created with a wiki. A wiki is software that allows users to create and edit web page content using any web browser. Because Wikipedia consists of 'open' information, anyone can change the entries or create new ones—in this way, Wikipedia is an example of **collaborative writing**.

1 Tick (✓) any correct answer. What is Wikipedia generally considered useful for?

a a starting point for research and information ______

b finding people's opinions ______

c a place to locate background information on a topic ______

d a place that will provide links or sources for further research ______

e a place to find late breaking news ______

f academic research ______

g finding information on new technology ______

h finding information on popular culture ______

Structure of a wiki article

Contents, headings and underlining are used to **organise** and **structure information** to make it visually and conceptually accessible.

A wiki site will use many **headings** and **subheadings** to assist in the location of information and topics. These headings are generally broad at the top and are followed by increasingly precise subheadings. Titles will be short, usually fewer than ten words.

2 Is this information about **structure** true of the Oodgeroo Noonuccal Wikipedia page? Support your answer with examples.

3 Note down five words that are blue in the Oodgeroo Noonuccal Wikipedia page. What do you notice about the blue words?

The blue words in the Wikipedia page are called **hypertext links** because they provide links and additional connections to information associated with the topic. Hypertext links are used to provide **emphasis**.

4 After reading the Oodgeroo Noonuccal Wikipedia page, what **hypertext links** would you need to click on in order to support your understanding of the article?

The Talk and History tabs

Every Wikipedia article has a related **Talk** and **History** page that can be accessed by tabs at the top of each entry. This technology provides an opportunity to trace the discussion of topics.

The Talk page is where Wikipedians go to 'talk' about articles. As the name suggests it offers a place for **discussion**, **critiquing** and **proposals**.

The History page is a chronological listing of every change and alteration made to an entry since its first incarnation.

5 What do you think are the benefits of being able to access this type of information?

Extend your skills

Conduct some further research on Oodgeroo Noonuccal using sources other than Wikipedia. Use the **effective web searching strategies** you explored in the first section of this chapter. If you were going to contribute to the Wikipedia page above on Oodgeroo, what would you add? Record your research here.

UNIT FOUR

Gothic fiction

Before you read

Reading **biographical information** about authors is useful for providing insight into the author's life, experiences and context. Read the following biographical information on Edgar Allan Poe and then answer the questions.

About the author Edgar Allan Poe

Edgar Allan Poe was an American poet, fiction writer and critic, best known as the father of the modern detective novel and for his unforgettable tales of terror. He was born in Boston, Massachusetts in 1809, the son of two poverty stricken actors. Poe's talent for writing was evident at an early age and his first published works were collections of poems. After studying Latin and poetry at Virginia University and a period in the army, he moved to Baltimore and continued to write, working for newspapers to earn a living. He then started to submit short stories to magazines and his first book of stories, *Tales of the Grotesque and Arabesque*, was published in 1839. Throughout his life, Poe struggled with poverty, alcohol and mental illness. In 1849, he was found unconscious in the street after a bout of heavy drinking. He did not recover. Poe's reputation continued to grow after his death and his books became especially popular in Europe. His work is still popular and very widely read today.

1 What do you think is the most important piece of information you learn about the author Edgar Allan Poe from this **biographical information**?

2 How do you feel about the author after reading the extract?

3 Based on the title of Poe's first book of stories, *Tales of the Grotesque and Arabesque,* what kind of stories do you think he wrote? Use a dictionary to define *grotesque* and *arabesque* if you need to.

Now read the text and answer the questions which follow. The text might be difficult to follow as the sentences tend to be long, have rather old-fashioned language patterns and are filled with images. You may need to read it more than once.

An extract from *The Fall of the House of Usher* by Edgar Allan Poe

During the whole of a dull, dark, and soundless day in the autumn of the year, when the clouds hung oppressively low in the heavens, I had been passing alone, on horseback, through a singularly dreary tract of country, and at length found myself, as the shades of the evening drew on, within view of the melancholy House of Usher. I know not how it was—but, with the first glimpse of the building, a sense of insufferable gloom pervaded my spirit. I say insufferable; for the feeling was unrelieved by any of that half-pleasurable, because poetic, sentiment, with which the mind usually receives even the sternest natural images of the desolate or terrible. I looked upon the scene before me—upon the mere house, and the simple landscape features of the domain—upon the bleak walls—upon the vacant eye-like windows—upon a few rank sedges—and upon a few white trunks of decayed trees—with an utter depression of soul which I can compare to no earthly sensation more properly than to the after-dream of the reveller upon opium—the bitter lapse into every-day life—the hideous dropping off of the veil. There was an iciness, a sinking, a sickening of the heart—an unredeemed dreariness of thought which no goading of the imagination could torture into aught of the sublime.

What was it—I paused to think—what was it that so unnerved me in the contemplation of the House of Usher? It was a mystery all insoluble; nor could I grapple with the shadowy fancies that crowded upon me as I pondered. I was forced to fall back upon the unsatisfactory conclusion, that while, beyond doubt, there are combinations of very simple natural objects which have the power of thus affecting us, still the analysis of this power lies among considerations beyond our depth. It was possible, I reflected, that a mere different arrangement of the particulars of the scene, of the details of the picture, would be sufficient to modify, or perhaps to annihilate its capacity for sorrowful impression; and, acting upon this idea, I reined my horse to the precipitous brink of a black and lurid tarn that lay in unruffled lustre by the dwelling, and gazed down—but with a shudder even more thrilling than before—upon the remodelled and inverted images of the gray sedge, and the ghastly tree-stems, and the vacant and eye-like windows.

Source: http://www.gutenberg.org/files/932/old/usher10h.htm

Test your understanding

1 The title of the story employs a technique called foreshadowing, whereby a clue or prediction is given about the story. After considering the title of the story, *The Fall of the House of Usher,* label the following potential events in the story either Possible (P) or Unlikely (U).

- **a** Usher is the name of a family. ______
- **b** The house belongs to the Usher family. ______
- **c** The house is going to fall over. ______
- **d** The story is set during Fall. ______
- **e** The Usher family will meet with a tragedy. ______
- **f** Usher is the name of a business owner. ______

2 'Poe creates right from the very beginning a general atmosphere of horror.' Find three examples of **ideas** from only the first four lines to support this. The first one has been done for you.

a dull, dark, and soundless day

b ______

c ______

d ______

3 Tick (✓) the correct answer. The atmosphere is created mostly through descriptions of which element?

a character ______

b feeling ______

c sound ______

d setting ______

4 Tick (✓) the correct answer. Where is the story set?

a in a rural location ______

b in a city ______

c in the modern age ______

d in a village street ______

5 Tick (✓) the correct answer. In the fourth line, which word could replace *singularly* in 'through a singularly dreary tract of country'?

a frequently ______

b bizarrely ______

c especially ______

d individually ______

6 The narrator tells the reader that 'with the first glimpse of the building, a sense of insufferable gloom pervaded my spirit.' Using your own words, what is the narrator's reaction to first seeing the house?

______

______

______

______

7 Tick (✓) the correct answer. When the narrator says 'that a mere different arrangement of the particulars of the scene, of the details of the picture, would be sufficient to modify or perhaps to annihilate its capacity for sorrowful impression', what do you think he means?

a that he would like to arrange the furniture and paint a picture of the house ______

b that the house could be even more bleak and depressing ______

c that changing some details of the house would lessen its terrible effect ______

d that changing some details of the house could increase its terrible effect ______

8 Match the following words from the story to their definition. You may need to use a dictionary.

tarn	conquer, overpower, crush
sedge	provoking, pushing, stirring
lurid	a person loudly enjoying themselves
annihilate	lake, pond, body of water
reveller	garish, striking, vivid
goading	awe-inspiring, overwhelming
sublime	grass-like plant that grows in wet areas

9 Circle five words from the list below that best describe how the house makes the narrator feel.

melancholy depressed secretive icy unsatisfied unnerved horrified

10 Use the textual clues in the excerpt from *The Fall of the House of Usher* to draw a picture of the house. It does not have to be fancy or elaborate but make sure you include the specific features given.

11 Which time period do you think the story is set in?

a 1800s

b 1900s

c 2000s

d 2100s

12 Justify the reasons for your answer in the previous question.

13 Do you want to continue reading the story? Why/Why not?

Boost your reading skills

Understanding how narratives begin

A **narrative orientation** is something that occurs at the beginning of a story and usually introduces the story's characters and setting. Orientations engage readers by **making connections** with the readers' expectations and thoughts. You may be familiar with the common opening sentence, *Once upon a time*, and as a result anticipate the story's development and conclusion.

Orientations create **visual pictures** of **settings** and **characters** in the readers' minds; they **portray** the **emotions** felt by characters, and can even get you thinking about your **perceptions** of yourself and your environment.

1 Complete the following table using examples from *The Fall of the House of Usher.* The first one has been done for you.

Features of orientations	**A general example (not from the Poe story)**	**Example from *The Fall of the House of Usher***
Physical or emotional response	My heart pounded and my knees knocked. I couldn't breathe from fear.	I looked upon the scene before me ... with an utter depression of soul. ... nor could I grapple with the shadowy fancies that crowded upon me as I pondered.
Image of setting	The barren earth crumbled, dry and lifeless under my shoes.	
Image of character	His eyes stared vacantly from two dark-ringed sockets.	
Questioning that challenges readers' thoughts	So, who do you think you are anyway, coming over like this, uninvited and unwanted?	

2 In the excerpt from *The Fall of the House of Usher* there is very little physical description of the narrator. What do you think is the effect of the author's deliberate **lack** of **description** of the narrator?

Work on words

Gothic vocabulary

Gothic fiction (sometimes referred to as Gothic horror) is a genre of literature that combines features of both **horror** and **romance**. Features of Gothic fiction include terror (both psychological and physical), mystery, barren landscapes, ghosts, haunted houses, castles, death, deterioration, madness, secrets and hereditary curses.

Edgar Allen Poe **creates atmosphere** through his selection of words that are particular to the gothic genre. Well-chosen words maintain the dark and haunted feeling that gothic stories are famous for. Edgar Allan Poe is considered an important and innovative interpreter of the Gothic. He is famous for focusing on the psychology of his characters and how they often descended into madness.

Another book that is generally regarded as the first gothic novel is *The Castle of Otranto*, a 1764 novel by Horace Walpole. The book began a literary genre which would become extremely popular in the later 18th century and early 19th century. His story is noticeable for vocabulary that communicates feelings of **mystery** about the unknown, creates **urgency** and instils **terror** in his readers.

Read the following sentences from *The Castle of Otranto*. Look at the examples below of words that are typical to **Gothic fiction** and place them in the sentence to which they belong. You may need to use a dictionary to check definitions.

1 Mark each with *M* for a word that communicates **mystery**, *U* for a word that communicates **urgency** or *T* for a word that communicates **terror**. The first one has been done for you.

anxious dread curdled fear rushed subterraneous suddenly

- **a** Looking with anxious fondness at Matilda, a silent tear stole down her cheek … U
- **b** Her blood ______; she concluded it was Manfred. ______
- **c** In this resolution, she seized a lamp that burned at the foot of the staircase, and hurried towards the ______ passage. ______
- **d** Rising ______, his face bedewed with tears, he would have ______ from her presence. ______
- **e** Her ______ of Manfred soon outweighed every other ______. ______

2 Read *The Fall of the House of Usher* extract again and highlight the following elements in the extract. Then write the words down in the table. The first few have been done for you.

Words in the story	Examples
Words associated with horror	dark, decayed, torture, precipitous

Words in the story	Examples
Words that show the narrator's fear	alone, sinking, sickening
Words used to describe the house	bleak, vacant

3 How does the writer provoke fear and anticipation in the reader through the use of **description**?

Spotlight on language

Creating suspense

The Fall of the House of Usher is a typical Gothic story with its features of a haunted house and bleak atmosphere.

However, instead of providing information about place and time, Edgar Allan Poe uses traditional **Gothic features** such as severe and foul weather and a barren, desolate landscape.

The story begins without complete explanation of the narrator's motives for arriving at the house of Usher, and this uncertainty sets the tone for the story's plot. The story opens and ends on this mysterious note and leaves many questions unanswered.

Edgar Allen Poe's literary techniques include:

- **suspense**—this is anxiety or apprehension resulting from an **uncertain**, undecided or mysterious situation.

1 What is the narrator in *The Fall of the House of Usher* **uncertain** about?

2 How does Poe create feelings of **suspense** in the reader towards the house?

* **pacing**—this is when an author advances or develops events at a particular rate or tempo

3 Would you describe the **pacing** of the story as fast or slow? Explain your choice.

* **a potential for dangerous/unpredictable action**—this is where the narrator's violent moods can create trouble for everyone, including himself

4 What indications from the extract inform you that the narrator is **troubled** and **potentially** in **danger**?

* **foreshadowing**—a literary device in which the author gives clues as to what will happen later

5 We know that the story's title **foreshadows** events about the story. In the excerpt are there any other examples of hints or suggestions about what might occur later on in the story?

- **repetition**—the deliberate repetition of ideas in order to achieve an artistic effect.
  For example:
  I looked upon the scene before me—upon the mere house, and the simple landscape features of the domain—upon the bleak walls—upon the vacant eye-like windows—upon a few rank sedges—and upon a few white trunks of decayed trees.

6 What is the effect of this **repetition**?

____

____

____

____

Symbolism in gothic fiction

Symbolism is used to represent **ideas** and **qualities** by suggesting meanings that are different from their literal sense. Generally, symbolism occurs when an object represents another to give it an entirely different meaning that is much deeper and more significant.

Symbols can shift their meanings depending on the **context** they are used in. A heart, for example, may stand for 'love' (e.g. in a narrative or a poem) as well as 'heart disease' (e.g. in a medical text). In gothic fiction, symbolism is used to represent themes such as death, deterioration, madness and secrets.

7 Place a word or an idea in the following table that explains what each feature of gothic stories may **symbolise**. The first two have been done for you.

Feature of gothic stories	What it symbolises
wailing winds	sorrow
strong rain	isolation
ruins of buildings	
baying of distant wolves	
absence of sound	
approaching footsteps	
thunder and lightning	

Extend your skills

The story you have just read is an excerpt (selection) from Edgar Allen Poe's *The Fall of the House of Usher* and not the whole story. The original and complete version of the story contains an **epigraph.** An epigraph is a short quotation or saying at the beginning of a book or chapter, intended to highlight its **theme**. Epigraphs are like little entrées to the main course of a story. They suggest important aspects of the story and they get you thinking about the story's **main ideas**.

Read this epigraph from *The Fall of the House of Usher* and answer the questions.
'The heart is a poised (waiting/ready) lute; as soon as it is touched, it resounds.'

1. A lute is a stringed instrument, like a guitar, that has a pear-shaped body. Why do you think the writer might compare a heart with a musical instrument like this?

2. What do you think the word *resounds* means in this sentence?

3. Now you know more about the story, can you predict what some of the **main themes** or **ideas** of the story may be from this **epigraph** and the excerpt you have read?

UNIT FIVE

Travel writing

Before you read

It is always easier to understand what you are reading if you have some **background knowledge** and **experience** of the topic. Activating this knowledge and experience helps you make connections between new and known information.

1 Define what *bush medicine* means to you.

2 What do you think the title *Rough Guides* communicates about the type of travel that will be discussed by a travel writer?

Rough Guides Learning the Ancient Art of Bush Medicine, Australia

1 In a country where a small spider can kill you, it's reassuring to know Mother Nature has a softer side. Hidden in the prehistoric valleys of the Blue Mountains National Park in New South Wales are hundreds of plants used by Aboriginal peoples to cure everything from earache and fevers, to snake bites and colds. The best chance you have of spotting them and learning about the art of bush medicine is to delve deep into the forest with an expert guide. Walking ancient hunting tracks used by indigenous peoples, far from the car parks and crowded viewpoints, you will discover a different side to this wonderful national park.

2 One of the first things you are struck by as you descend into the chiseled gorges of the park is the smell—an astringent mix of eucalyptus and tea tree, a result of the oils evaporating from these plants which also gives the air its blue haze. While you might think of tea-tree oil being used to zap the odd spot, Aboriginals used it widely, inhaling the infused oil to cure coughs and stuffing the raw leaves into cuts to prevent infection. Colonial settlers soon learnt about this miracle plant and tea-tree oil was even issued to Australian soldiers in WWII.

3 Descending further, the hum of cicadas gets louder and the air becomes humid as you enter the moss- and lichen-encrusted cloud forest. While you concentrate on the barely distinguishable path, your eagle-eyed guide will point out everything from bush pears, an ancient Aboriginal snack, to the aptly named headache vine, once crushed and rubbed directly into the skin to treat migraines. As the gradient steepens, you're glad of the guide ropes attached to the slippery

stone walls. Nonetheless, most people end up with an impromptu mud pack on their lower half before they reach the bottom of the creek. As the air grows warmer and your spirits start to flag, your ears will welcome the hiss of the nearby Wentworth Falls, signaling both the hike's end point and the prospect of an invigorating swim.

Source: http://www.roughguides.com/article/learning-the-ancient-art-of-bush-medicine-australia/

Test your understanding

1 Tick (✓) the correct answer. What does the line 'it's reassuring to know Mother Nature has a softer side' mean?

- **a** Australia's landscape can be really harsh and dangerous. ______
- **b** Nature is kinder in Australia than in other countries. ______
- **c** Australia's environment offers reassurance to its visitors. ______
- **d** Australia's landscape contains remedies and cures as well as dangers. ______

2 Tick (✓) the correct answer. In the line 'The best chance you have of … learning about the art of bush medicine is to delve deep into the forest with an expert guide', which word could best replace *delve*?

- **a** gaze ______
- **b** evaluate ______
- **c** dig ______
- **d** explore ______

3 Tick (✓) the correct answer. What is the 'different' side to this wonderful national park you will discover?

- **a** walking ancient hunting tracks ______
- **b** discovering medicinal plants ______
- **c** visiting Blue Mountains National Park ______
- **d** observing prehistoric valleys ______

4 Tick (✓) the correct answer. Tea tree oil comes from

- **a** eucalypts. ______
- **b** evaporating oils. ______
- **c** a mixture of eucalyptus and tea tree. ______
- **d** the tea tree plant. ______

5 Tick (✓) the correct answer. Colonial settlers called tea tree a 'miracle' plant because

- **a** it had spiritual significance to indigenous people. ______
- **b** it is useful in a variety of situations. ______
- **c** they had never seen it before. ______
- **d** it is good for clearing up pimples. ______

6 Tick (✓) the correct answer. The line 'Descending further, the hum of cicadas gets louder and the air becomes humid as you enter the moss- and lichen-encrusted cloud forest' stimulates which senses for the reader?

- **a** sight ______
- **b** sound and sight ______
- **c** sound, sight and feel ______
- **d** feel and sound ______

7 In the final paragraph, is the track you are walking on established and well trodden or haphazard and unclear? Find a quote to support your response.

____

____

____

____

____

8 Tick (✓) the correct answer. Why do most people 'end up with an impromptu mud pack on their lower half before they reach the bottom of the creek'?

- **a** Despite support, it's difficult to stand on the slippery slope. ______
- **b** People deliberately pack mud on their legs as a beauty treatment. ______
- **c** The mud is waist-high where they are walking. ______
- **d** a and c ______

9 Tick (✓) any correct answer. The purpose of the travel article is to

- **a** persuade people to visit the Blue Mountains National park. ______
- **b** inform people about walking tours. ______
- **c** shed light on Indigenous culture within the Blue Mountains region. ______
- **d** a, b and c. ______

10 Look back at these words from the text and underline the best definition. You should use the context of the sentence to help you work out the meaning.

a *astringent* (paragraph 2):	sharp	clear	pleasant
b *chiselled* (paragraph 2):	specific	sculptured	determined
c *infused* (paragraph 2):	added	woven	swallowed
d *encrusted* (paragraph 3):	coated	blotchy	tainted
e *aptly* (paragraph 3):	handily	gracefully	fittingly
f *gradient* (paragraph 3):	elevation	incline	summit
g *impromptu* (paragraph 3):	deliberate	spontaneous	planned

Boost your reading skills

Skimming for the main idea

Skimming is a reading technique that involves rapidly moving your eyes over the text with the purpose of gaining a **general overview** and the **main idea**.

Skimming can be used during the three main types of reading you do:

- **pre-reading**—skimming can provide a general overview of what is about to be read
- **during reading**—skimming is useful for quickly reading information that does not require close and thorough reading
- **reviewing**—skimming is a good tool for going over information already read

When you skim you should look at titles, headings and subheadings, any highlighted words (e.g. words in **bold**, or words underlined), and first sentences of paragraphs. You should also take notice of any words or phrases that occur frequently in the text.

1 Quickly **skim** the text below (take no longer than two seconds). In your own words, and without looking again, what do you think the article will be about?

Bush medicine—methodology

1 Generally, bush medicine is made from plant materials such as bark, leaves and seeds. Sometimes however animal products were used as well. Except for ointments, which were made by mixing crushed leaves with animal fat, medicines were rarely mixed. Very occasionally two plants were used together.

2 In general, there are two types of accepted causes of illness in aboriginal tribes—natural, and supernatural. Natural causes would be treated with natural remedies, and supernatural illnesses could only be treated with a spiritual cure. It was believed that evil spirits caused any illness without an obvious explanation and these would be treated by the tribe's medicine man who would specialise in spiritual cures. The medicine men mainly use bush animal dung or plants in their medicine.

3 Aboriginal remedies varied between clans in different parts of the country. There was no single set of Aboriginal medicines and remedies, just as there was no one Aboriginal language.

4 Traditions in southern and eastern Australia have largely been lost. However efforts are being made by anthropologists to record traditions from Aborigines in central and north-western Australia. The adoption of many introduced plants into bush medicine suggests the possibility that many of the native remedies would have changed through time.

2 Now read only the first sentences of the paragraphs. Underline the **key words** in each. These are normally nouns (things) and verbs (action words) that are important to the topic.

For example: in paragraph 1—Generally, bush medicine is made from plant materials such as bark, leaves and seeds.

3 On the basis of the first sentences only, decide what the topics of each paragraph will be.

a Paragraph 1: ____________________

b Paragraph 2: ____________________

c Paragraph 3: ____________________

d Paragraph 4: ____________________

4 Now **skim** read the whole text before reading it right through. Were your answers to Question 3 correct?

____

____

5 Read the first sentence of each paragraph, listed below. For each one, underline the **key words**. Then in your own words explain what the paragraph is about.

a In a country where a small spider can kill you, it's reassuring to know Mother Nature has a softer side.

____

____

____

____

b One of the first things you are struck by as you descend into the chiseled gorges of the park is the smell—an astringent mix of eucalyptus and tea tree, a result of the oils evaporating from these plants which also gives the air its blue haze.

____

____

____

____

c Descending further, the hum of cicadas gets louder and the air becomes humid as you enter the moss- and lichen-encrusted cloud forest.

____

____

____

____

6 Now **skim** the remaining information in each paragraph, underlining key words as you skim. What are the **main ideas** of the article you have just read?

____

____

Don't forget—**skimming** becomes easier the more you do it. It may seem time consuming at first as you are required to look for particular and specific information, but as you grow more familiar with what you are looking for, the process itself will become faster and more efficient.

Work on words

Collocations

A **collocation** is two or more words that frequently go together. These combinations sound normal to native English speakers who use them all the time. On the other hand, incorrect combinations sound 'wrong'.

For example: We say *burst into tears* but we don't say *split into tears*. We say *crystal clear* but we don't say *glass clear*.

1 Underline the most **commonly used** phrases from the following pairs.

- **a** a fast shower/a quick shower
- **b** quick food/fast food
- **c** tall ceiling/high ceiling

2 Look at the following sentences and in each case underline the word which makes the **collocation**.

- **a** I love a good cup of strong/powerful tea.
- **b** Outlet stores are big/large business these days.
- **c** During the event I needed to make small/little talk with other people.
- **d** She didn't like it when people made a big/large deal about her birthday.
- **e** The leader decided to take/grip control of the situation.
- **f** She decided she didn't really want to get married to/with him after all.
- **g** We have had some strong/heavy rain this week.

3 Look at the following words and phrases and add either of the verbs *do* or *make* to each example. The first two have been done for you.

- **a** __make__ a mistake
- **b** __do__ the housework
- **c** ________ the beds
- **d** ________ a wish
- **e** ________ a test
- **f** ________ your hair

g __________ some damage

h __________ a phone call

i __________ a noise

j __________ a promise

Collocations of *side*

The travel article uses two collocations which include the noun *side* in order to describe the different features of the national park.

For example: '… it's reassuring to know Mother Nature has a **softer side**.'

'… you will discover a **different side** to this wonderful national park.'

In the two examples above, *side* refers to an 'aspect' or 'perspective' rather than a physical location. As with all collocations there are other words that might have been used to convey the same meanings, but these would not have been collocations. We say someone has *a soft side* but we don't usually say someone has *a mild side* or *an easy side*. We talk about *a different side* but we don't talk about *a dissimilar side* or *a separate side*.

4 The word *side* is used with many other words in **collocations**. Use each of the following *side* collocations in the correct sentence. The first one has been done for you.

other side	downside	offside	weaker side
each side	safe side	bright side	wrong side

a We live on the other side of town to you.

b He came from the ______________ of the tracks.

c The ______________ will be the lack of resources available.

d Place the cutlery on ______________ of the plate.

e The player was considered ______________ by the referee.

f Despite appearing strong, there was a ______________ to his personality.

g He always looked on the ______________ despite his many problems.

h To be on the ______________, we had locked all the doors.

Spotlight on language

Multisensory description

A **sensory description** is one that describes objects so that the reader can relate the experience to one of their five senses: **olfactory** (smell), **gustatory** (taste), **tactile** (touch), **visual** (sight) and **auditory** (hearing). These allow the writer to communicate their experience to the reader in real and vivid ways.

The *Rough Guides* author uses a variety of sensory descriptions to bring their travel article to life and to communicate a realistic sense of the travel experience to the reader. The sensory descriptions may also encourage readers to visit the location themselves.

1 Take a look at the following examples from the *Rough Guides* text. Underline the **sensory description** and then identify the sense that is being stimulated. Some sentences may contain more than one example.

a Descending further, the hum of cicadas gets louder and the air becomes humid as you enter the moss- and lichen-encrusted cloud forest.

Senses stimulated: auditory, tactile, visual

b While you concentrate on the barely distinguishable path, your eagle-eyed guide will point out everything from bush pears, an ancient Aboriginal snack, to the aptly named headache vine, once crushed and rubbed directly into the skin to treat migraines.

Senses stimulated: ____________ and ____________

c As the air grows warmer and your spirits start to flag, your ears will welcome the hiss of the nearby Wentworth Falls, signaling both the hike's end point and the prospect of an invigorating swim.

Senses stimulated: ____________ and ____________

d One of the first things you are struck by as you descend into the chiseled gorges of the park is the smell—an astringent mix of eucalyptus and tea tree, a result of the oils evaporating from these plants which also gives the air its blue haze.

Senses stimulated: ____________ and ____________

e Walking ancient hunting tracks used by indigenous peoples, far from the car parks and crowded viewpoints, you will discover a different side to this wonderful national park.

Senses stimulated: ____________

When writing, you want the reader to experience what you have experienced. Telling an audience something looks beautiful or tastes good is not enough—you need to create images that stimulate ideas about your experience and this can be achieved through **sensory imagery**.

2 Below are the beginning sentences of a paragraph that describe a summer holiday in Queensland. The scene leaves the reader with many unanswered questions. Without the inclusion of **sensory detail**, the writing seems to lack colour and is unexciting and non-specific. How might you use **descriptive detail** to make the scene more vivid?
The day was hot and stormy. We visited the beach in the morning and then hung around the hotel pool in the afternoon.

a **Add sight**—what do you see?

For example:
The day was hot and stormy. Low grey clouds, pregnant with water, hung ominously in the darkened sky like ghostly galleons.

What else can you see?

____

____

____

b **Add sound**—what do you hear?

For example:
We heard … / The sound of …

____

____

c **Add smell**—what do you smell?

For example:
The storm smelled of ...

d **Add touch**—what do you feel?

For example:
The rain felt like ... /The swimming pool water was ...

e **Add taste**—what can you taste?

For example:
The air tasted of ... /The rain tasted like ...

Now put your ideas together and write the descriptive paragraph.

Extend your skills

Use the scaffold below to help you write about a recent travel experience. You may have travelled overseas, interstate or perhaps had a short weekend or day-trip away somewhere interesting. If not, you may like to write about a recent school excursion.

Travel writing:

- is personal and may use **first-person narration** (*I*, *me* or *we*)
- has a strong sense of the writer's **personality**
- uses **personal experiences** and **anecdotes**
- is **vivid** and creates clear pictures in the reader's head through **multi-sensory descriptions**
- uses **facts** about places being described.

1 Describe the place

For example:
is typical of/distinctive/an unusual example of/The street, which is crowded during holidays

2 Offer advice or recommendations about an aspect of your experience

For example:
Stop over/Don't miss/Go/Walk/Eat at/On no account/Make certain ...

3 Offer suggestions

For example:
If you like/then/is ideal for/Take care/If you're looking for/If you have young children, then

4 Review the overall experience

For example:
spectacular/thought-provoking/attractive/the best example of its kind/worth visiting

UNIT SIX

Shakespeare

Before you read

Making predictions is more than just guessing what is going to happen next. Predicting helps you become **actively involved** while you read a text and will assist you to **form judgements** and **opinions** about what you are reading.

Think about this while you read the following plot summary.

Othello

Othello is a highly esteemed general in the service of Venice, Italy, during the 1500's. Iago is Othello's ambitious friend and comrade. However, when Othello promotes Michael Cassio, from Florence, to the position of personal lieutenant, Iago becomes deadly jealous. Iago begins an evil and malicious campaign against the hero. When Othello marries Desdemona Iago starts to plot against them. He uses Cassio to make it appear that Desdemona is being unfaithful, and as a result, Othello becomes jealous and suspicious of Desdemona.

1 Shakespeare's plays fall into three main categories: comedy, tragedy and histories. Based on the summary above, what category do you think *Othello* will fall into and why?

____

____

2 Write definitions for the following key words from the above summary of the plot. They are important to understanding the play's main themes.

a ambitious ______________________________

b malicious ______________________________

c plot ______________________________

d jealous ______________________________

An excerpt from Shakespeare's *Othello*—Act 2, Scene 3

Original text	Modern interpretation
IAGO	IAGO
And what's he then that says I play the villain? When this advice is free I give and honest, Probal to thinking and indeed the course To win the Moor again? For 'tis most easy Th' inclining Desdemona to subdue In any honest suit. She's framed as fruitful As the free elements. And then for her To win the Moor, were to renounce his baptism, All seals and symbols of redeemèd sin, His soul is so enfettered to her love, That she may make, unmake, do what she list,	Who can say I'm evil when my assistance is so useful? That's really the best way to persuade the Moor back. It's simple to get Desdemona on your side. She's full of good meanings. And the Moor adores her so much he would reject his Christianity to keep her content. He's so imprisoned by love that she can force him to do whatever she wants.

Even as her appetite shall play the god With his weak function. How am I then a villain To counsel Cassio to this parallel course, Directly to his good? Divinity of hell! When devils will the blackest sins put on They do suggest at first with heavenly shows As I do now. For whiles this honest fool Plies Desdemona to repair his fortune And she for him pleads strongly to the Moor, I'll pour this pestilence into his ear: That she repeals him for her body's lust. And by how much she strives to do him good She shall undo her credit with the Moor. So will I turn her virtue into pitch And out of her own goodness make the net That shall enmesh them all.	How am I evil to advise Cassio to do exactly what'll benefit him? That's the kind of disagreement you'd expect from Satan! When devils are about to commit their most serious sins they put on their most heavenly faces, just as I'm doing now. And while this fool is pleading Desdemona to help him, and while she's supporting him to the Moor, I'll poison the Moor's ear against her, hinting that she's on Cassio's side because of her desire for him. The more she tries to help Cassio, the more she'll undermine Othello's assurance in her. And that's how I'll turn her good objectives into a snare to trick them all.

Test your understanding

Use the modern interpretation of the text to help you answer the questions if you need to.

1 Tick (✓) the correct answer.

The above text is known as a soliloquy. Based on what you have read, which of the following best defines the term?

a a conversation between characters heard only by those characters speaking ______

b an 'off stage' performance that is heard by other characters ______

c the act of speaking one's thoughts aloud when by oneself or regardless of any hearers ______

d a speech delivered to the play audience only ______

2 Match the character's names to their descriptions.

Othello	the speaker, a character with evil intentions
Desdemona	a character who Iago will use to undermine Desdemona's strong reputation
Iago	Othello's wife and the person Iago will manipulate in order to seek revenge against
Cassio	'the Moor'; in other words, a person who comes from North Africa

3 Tick (✓) the correct answer. Why does Iago choose Othello's wife Desdemona as a means to seek his revenge on Othello?

a He is secretly in love with her and hopes to marry her in the future. ______

b Othello loves her so deeply that she may easily influence him. ______

c His anger and jealousy is directed towards Desdemona as well. ______

d This scenario will assist him to advance within the military. ______

4 Tick (✓) the correct answer. Given Iago's character, the line 'When this advice is free I give and honest' is:

a humorous. It makes the audience laugh ______

b ironic. Iago is clearly not 'honest'. ______

c deceptive. Iago wants to be honest and liked. ______

d factual. Iago provides assistance with good intentions. ______

5 Tick (✓) the correct answer. Who is the 'honest fool' Iago refers to?

a himself ______

b Othello ______

c Desdemona ______

d Cassio ______

6 Tick (✓) the correct answer. What are Desdemona's 'good intentions'?

a to assist Iago to achieve his aims ______

b to help her husband advance in military rank ______

c to encourage her husband to look positively on Iago ______

d to help Cassio gain favour with her husband ______

7 Using your own words, explain the following line: 'So I will turn her virtue into pitch'.

____

____

8 Tick (✓) the correct answer. Which line best shows why Othello will be suspicious of his wife Desdemona?

a And she for him pleads strongly to the Moor ______

b His soul is so enfettered to her love ______

c So will I turn her virtue into pitch ______

d That she repeals him for her body's lust ______

9 Shakespeare's plays still resonate strongly with modern audiences, despite being over 500 years old. Why do you think this play, *Othello,* is still so popular today?

____

____

Boost your reading skills

Understanding Shakespearean language

Shakespeare doesn't always read like 'normal' English because he wrote for an audience over 400 years ago. Even if you are confused about some words and phrases, you should still be able to pick up meaning from the context (circumstances), and reading the play out loud may help the language sound more natural. Readers who familiarise themselves with these **common Shakespearean words** will be rewarded by a smoother reading of the plays.

1 Here is a list of some of the most common words in Shakespeare's plays with which you might not be familiar. Match the following underlined words in the sentences to their **modern meaning** on the right. The sentences should provide a clue to their meaning. The first one has been done for you.

a Anon, good nurse! Speak!	exclamation of disgust
b Thou art dead; no physician's art can save you.	right now
c Dost thou know the time?	before
d We must leave ere daybreak.	are
e I fain would bake my teacher a cake if I could get an A.	does or do
f You cheated? Fie upon it! (upon you?)	gladly

2 Match the sentences on the left with the correct **Shakespearean words** in the column on the right. The first one has been done for you.

a Listen to the bird	hath
b Come here young lad	hark
c He has a horse	whence
d You are a villain	hither
e Your name is more hateful than your face	art
f Return to where you came	whyfore
g Why dost thou leave?	thy

William Shakespeare is also known for the retorts, verbal abuse and insults that he used in his plays. Some of Shakespeare's most thrilling moments include the carefully constructed **verbal attacks** his characters throw at one another during moments of heightened drama in his plays.

Look at the following examples from his plays:

Heaven truly knows that thou art false as hell (*Othello*)

3 What is Othello saying about Iago's character?

Thou art like a toad; ugly and venomous (*As You Like It*)

4 Why is being called a 'toad' insulting?

That trunk of humours, that bolting-hutch of beastliness, that swollen parcel of dropsies, that huge bombard of sack, that stuffed cloak-bag of guts, that roasted Manningtree ox with pudding in his belly, that reverend vice, that grey Iniquity, that father ruffian, that vanity in years? (*King Henry IV, Part 1*)

5 What visual impression does this insult give you?

6 Have some fun with Shakespeare and combine one word from each of the three columns below to create your own Shakespearean insults. Preface each example with *Thou*.

For example:
Thou mewling dizzy-eyed maggot-pie.

artless	cream-faced	toad
loathsome	fat	guts
beslubbering	fool	maggot-pie
bootless	beetle-headed	bladder
surly	boil-brained	boar-pig
cockered	half-faced	mongrel
mewling	scullian	strumpet
craven	common-kissing	canker-blossom
puke-stocking	stewed	prune
puking	embossed	carbuncle
spongy	dizzy-eyed	measle
droning	doghearted	codpiece
lumpish	saucy	cut-throat
fawning	toss'd	weasel

Record your insults here.

Work on words

Modern Shakespearean words

The English language has changed a great deal over the last few hundred years, and it is continually evolving. Shakespeare himself created many new words and phrases, and as a result his language is a mixture of both the old and the new. Shakespeare introduced nearly 3000 words into the English language. In addition Shakespeare's works, which were often quoted, became so common that they helped set the standards for Modern English; prior to Shakespeare, English grammar and spelling followed few rules.

The list on the following page contains words that we use in our daily speech. These words were brought into **modern use by Shakespeare**—you may recognise some of them.

apostrophe	dishearten	inauspicious	obscene	seamy
auspicious	fitful	indistinguishable	perusal	submerge
baseless	frugal	invulnerable	pious	suspicious
castigate	gloomy	lapse	premeditated	
clangour	gnarled	monumental	road	
dexterously	impartial	multitudinous	sanctimonious	

1 The following sentences contain an underlined synonym for one of the words in the list. Locate the word from the list that matches the **synonym** and write it on the line. The first one has been done for you.

a The car breaking down was an ominous start to the week. inauspicious

b The woman was known as being sparing with her money. ______

c The policeman maintained an unprejudiced attitude towards the situation. ______

d The shopkeeper had organised around the shop many items for our inspection. ______

e I have let my passport expire and now need to apply for another. ______

f The allegations made by the criminal were judged to be unfounded. ______

g The politician was considered self-satisfied and smug. ______

2 Choose five more words from the list that you are unfamiliar with. Look up their meanings using a dictionary and use each in a sentence that best reflects their **modern meaning**.

a ______

b ______

c ______

d ______

e ______

3 The following phrases are from Shakespearean plays—you will notice that they are **commonly used** today. Think about the likely meaning and then fill in the blanks with one of the phrases.

the green-eyed monster	in his heart of hearts	pomp and circumstance
foregone conclusion	at one fell swoop	

a It's a ______ that a new Prime Minister will be elected.

b ______, he knew that he would have to sell the company.

c You shouldn't want what others have; you will turn into ______.

d ______, everything we had worked so hard to achieve was destroyed.

e The event continued with much ______.

Spotlight on language

Shakespearean techniques

Shakespeare used language in **poetic** and **highly descriptive** ways. In Elizabethan drama, sets were quite bare, with few props or accessories and so audiences needed to use their imaginations to create the scenery of the play. Shakespeare's use of language helped the audience to bring the play and its characters to rich and vibrant life. He achieved this by using a variety of **techniques**.

Opposite words or **ideas** occur often in *Othello*—they focus on themes in the plot such as appearance versus reality or good versus evil. An **oxymoron** is when words with opposing meanings are put together, like *fair devil*. These techniques are used to highlight a character's thoughts and feelings, as well as to reveal ideas about their personalities.

1 Look at the following examples from *Othello* and underline the **opposite ideas**. They may be placed next to each other or separately within the sentence. The first one has been done for you.

- **a** When devils will the blackest sins put on/They do suggest at first with heavenly shows
- **b** And what's he then that says I play the villain?/When this advice is free I give and honest
- **c** Divinity of hell!
- **d** For whiles this honest fool/Plies Desdemona to repair his fortune
- **e** Upon malicious bravery, dost thou come/To start my quiet
- **f** Excellent wretch! Perdition catch my soul

Imagery is used often in *Othello*. This is when strong pictures or ideas are created in our minds. In *Othello,* Shakespeare has created many references to darkness, to animals, to disease and to hell. Imagery is used to describe one thing in terms of another. **Metaphors** are an example of imagery.

For example: Iago says, 'Our bodies are our gardens' and makes different references to nature. He also calls Othello a 'Barbary horse' and later a 'ram'.

2 Look at the following examples from *Othello* and answer the questions:

a I'll pour this pestilence into his ear

'Pestilence' is a metaphor for information and ideas that Iago is 'pouring' into Othello's ears. What type of information is Iago giving Othello?

For example: is it information that will benefit someone or hurt someone? (Think about the meaning of 'pestilence'.)

____

____

____

b So will I turn her virtue into pitch

Desdemona's 'virtue' is her good reputation. What does Iago plan to do to her reputation? (What colour is 'pitch'? Think about the meaning of the phrase *pitch black*.)

____

____

c And out of her own goodness make the net / That shall enmesh them all.

What is the 'net' that Iago will create, and what will the 'net' do? (Think about nets—when and how are they sometimes dangerous?)

Extend your skills

Using language in your responses

When you write about Shakespeare and other texts you study it is preferable to include some discussion of **language**; otherwise you will simply be retelling the story.

1 Write a **short structured paragraph** of analysis on the *Othello* extract above, using the following scaffold.

1 The **topic sentence** contains the main idea of the paragraph, so use the language of the question. What are the **names** of the play, act and scene you are writing on? What is important about this extract? What does it **reveal about the character** of Iago?
2 Re-state the main idea by adding explanation. What are the **main themes** and **ideas** associated with this extract? Include at least ONE **quote** to support your ideas.
3 Give a language example to support your view. How does Shakespeare **communicate** the **main themes** of the extract? What **devices** does he use (e.g. **imagery** or **oxymoron**)?
4 Concluding sentence—sum up your ideas and return to the main idea of the paragraph. What are the **overall ideas** communicated by the *Othello* extract?

UNIT SEVEN

Political speech

Before you read

On 13 February 2008, the then Prime Minister Kevin Rudd apologised in parliament to Australia's Indigenous peoples, particularly the Stolen Generations and their families and communities. He apologised for laws and policies which had resulted in suffering and loss. The apology included a plan for a policy to reduce the differences between Indigenous and non-Indigenous Australians.

Thinking about what you know of the **topic** before you start reading a text will help you connect with the information and ideas it contains.

1 Who are the 'Stolen Generations'? If you aren't sure, make an educated guess after thinking about the name.

2 What does it mean to be 'indigenous'?

3 Why do you think the apology meant so much to Indigenous Australians?

An excerpt from Kevin Rudd's *Sorry Day* speech

An excerpt from Kevin Rudd's *Sorry Day* speech

1 To the stolen generations, I say the following: as Prime Minister of Australia, I am sorry. On behalf of the government of Australia, I am sorry. On behalf of the parliament of Australia, I am sorry. I offer you this apology without qualification. We apologise for the hurt, the pain and suffering that we, the parliament, have caused you by the laws that previous parliaments have enacted. We apologise for the indignity, the degradation

and the humiliation these laws embodied. We offer this apology to the mothers, the fathers, the brothers, the sisters, the families and the communities whose lives were ripped apart by the actions of successive governments under successive parliaments. In making this apology, I would also like to speak personally to the members of the stolen generations and their families: to those here today, so many of you; to those listening across the nation—from Yuendumu, in the central west of the Northern Territory, to Yabara, in North Queensland, and to Pitjantjatjara in South Australia.

2 I know that, in offering this apology on behalf of the government and the parliament, there is nothing I can say today that can take away the pain you have suffered personally. Whatever words I speak today, I cannot undo that. Words alone are not that powerful; grief is a very personal thing.

I ask those non-Indigenous Australians listening today who may not fully understand why what we are doing is so important to imagine for a moment that this had happened to you. I say to honourable members here present: imagine if this had happened to us. Imagine the crippling effect. Imagine how hard it would be to forgive. My proposal is this: if the apology we extend today is accepted in the spirit of reconciliation in which it is offered, we can today resolve together that there be a new beginning for Australia. And it is to such a new beginning that I believe the nation is now calling us.

3 Australians are a passionate lot. We are also a very practical lot. For us, symbolism is important but, unless the great symbolism of reconciliation is accompanied by an even greater substance, it is little more than a clanging gong. It is not sentiment that makes history; it is our actions that make history. Today's apology, however inadequate, is aimed at righting past wrongs. It is also aimed at building a bridge between Indigenous and non-Indigenous Australians—a bridge based on a real respect rather than a thinly veiled contempt. Our challenge for the future is to now cross that bridge and, in so doing, to embrace a new partnership between Indigenous and non-Indigenous Australians—embracing, as part of that partnership, expanded Link-Up and other critical services to help the stolen generations to trace their families if at all possible and to provide dignity to their lives. But the core of this partnership for the future is the closing of the gap between Indigenous and non-Indigenous Australians on life expectancy, educational achievement and employment opportunities. This new partnership on closing the gap will set concrete targets for the future: within a decade to halve the widening gap in literacy, numeracy and employment outcomes and opportunities for Indigenous Australians, within a decade to halve the appalling gap in infant mortality rates between Indigenous and non-Indigenous children and, within a generation, to close the equally appalling 17-year life gap between Indigenous and non-Indigenous in overall life expectancy.

Source: http://parlinfo.aph.gov.au/parlInfo/search/display/display.w3p;query=Id%3A%22chamber%2Fhansardr%2F2008-02-13%2F0003%22

Test your understanding

1 Tick (✓) the correct answer. When Kevin Rudd states in his opening paragraph 'I offer this apology without qualification', what does he mean?

a he apologises with doubt, with uncertainty ______

b he apologises completely, with no exceptions ______

c he apologises with accuracy, with precision ______

d he is qualified to offer this apology ______

2 Tick (✓) all correct answers. When Kevin Rudd uses the inclusive pronoun *we* in the opening paragraph, who is he referring to?

a all Australians ______

b the Prime Minister of Australia ______

c the Government and Parliament of Australia ______

d b and c ______

3 Tick (✓) the correct answer. The speech has emotional content and like many effective speeches, aims to evoke an emotional response. Which of the following groups of words taken from the speech do you think would create the highest emotional response in the listener?

a grief, spirit, challenge, beginning ______

b life expectancy, educational achievement, opportunities ______

c passionate, practical, symbolism, substance ______

d ripped apart, pain, suffering, humiliation ______

4 Tick (✓) the correct answer. What is the second paragraph's main message?

a Kevin Rudd's words can't change the past, but he hopes they will inspire a new beginning. ______

b Grief is very personal and each Indigenous Australian has their own story and experiences. ______

c Kevin Rudd wants his audience to imagine what the experience would have been like for them. ______

d Past events have made it very difficult for Indigenous Australians to be forgiving. ______

5 Tick (✓) the correct answer. What is another way to express the idea of the *spirit of reconciliation*?

a a religious connection between Indigenous and non-Indigenous Australians ______

b a longing to return to the past ______

c the potential to reunite Indigenous and non-Indigenous Australians ______

d a desire to resolve past problems and move forward ______

6 Tick (✓) the correct answer. Choose the sentence that best conveys Kevin Rudd's desire that reconciliation be meaningful.

a Australians are a passionate lot. We are also a very practical lot. ______

b … unless the great symbolism of reconciliation is accompanied by an even greater substance, it is little more than a clanging gong. ______

c If the apology we extend today is accepted in the spirit of reconciliation in which it is offered, we can today resolve together that there be a new beginning for Australia. ______

d Our challenge for the future is to now cross that bridge and, in so doing, to embrace a new partnership between Indigenous and non-Indigenous Australians. ______

7 Tick (✓) all correct answers. What is the purpose of this speech?

a to apologise to Australia's Indigenous community ______

b to reflect on Australian history ______

c to focus on ways to move forward ______

d a and c ______

8 Using your own words, what does 'closing the gap' mean in the final paragraph when Kevin Rudd says 'But the core of this partnership for the future is the closing of the gap between Indigenous and non-Indigenous Australians on life expectancy, educational achievement and employment opportunities?'

9 The *Sorry Day* speech is considered a significant event in recent Australian political history. Why do you believe it made such an impression on Australian society? What is its significance?

Boost your reading skills

Paraphrasing

A **paraphrase** is a restatement of a writer's original words. Paraphrasing is the most difficult form of note-taking as it involves taking someone else's ideas and writing them again using your own words. It is different to summarising. In summarising you reduce the content of what you are reading, but a paraphrase may be longer, shorter or even the same length as the original.

You should paraphrase when:

- you want to keep all the main points of what you are reading
- you want to communicate ideas using your own words while retaining the original meaning
- you want to avoid the risk of plagiarising (closely copying the language and thoughts of another author without authorisation).

A good paraphrase differs significantly from the wording of the original, without changing the essential **meaning** of the information.

There are two main techniques in paraphrasing:

- **changing** the **vocabulary**—this means finding **synonyms** (similar words) for key words in the text

  For example: suffering—adversity, enacted—endorsed, apologise—atone

1 Look at the following example from the *Sorry Day* speech. Find **synonyms** to replace the bold key words. You may need a thesaurus to help you. Remember: you don't want to alter the essential message of the sentence, so choose your synonyms carefully.

Australians are a **passionate** ______________ lot. We are also a very **practical** ______________ lot. For us, symbolism is important but, unless the great symbolism of **reconciliation** ______________ is accompanied by an even greater substance, it is little more than a **clanging gong** ______________.

We apologise for the **indignity** ______________, the **degradation** ______________ and the humiliation these laws **embodied** ______________.

Words alone are not that **powerful** ______________; grief is a very personal thing.

My proposal is this: if the apology we extend today is **accepted** ______________ in the spirit of reconciliation in which it is offered, we can today **resolve** ______________ together that there be a new beginning for Australia.

Today's apology, however **inadequate** ______________, is aimed at righting past **wrongs** ______________.

* **changing** the **word class**—this means turning adjectives into nouns, and vice versa. This is an effective way to paraphrase as it forces you to vary the ideas in a sentence.

The following examples show the noun and its paired adjective in *italics*.

health—*healthy* **speed**—*speedy* **wealth**—*wealthy* **extremity**—*extreme*
belief—*believable* **ease**—*easy* **strength**—*strong* **colour**—*colourful*

2 Find the **adjectival form** of the following nouns from the *Sorry Day* speech. The first one has been done for you.

Noun	Adjective
symbol	symbolic
apology	
degradation	
pain	
parliament	
humiliation	
substance	

3 Now use the table above to change the word class of the bolded **nouns** to **adjectives** and then rewrite the sentences. In doing this, the sentence may change significantly. The first one has been done for you.

a I know that, in offering this **apology** (adjective—*apologetic*) on behalf of the government and the parliament, there is nothing I can say today that can take away the **pain** (adjective—*painful*) you have suffered personally.

Answer: The government and the parliament are apologetic. There is nothing that they can say today that will lessen Indigenous Australia's painful experiences.

b We apologise for the hurt, the **pain** and suffering that we, the **parliament**, have caused you by the laws that previous parliaments have enacted.

Answer: ____

____

c We apologise for the indignity, the **degradation** and the humiliation these laws embodied.

Answer: ____________________

d For us, **symbolism** is important but, unless the great symbolism of reconciliation is accompanied by an even greater **substance**, it is little more than a clanging gong.

Answer: ____________________

4 **Paraphrase** the following sentence by changing both the **vocabulary** and the **word class**. (The nouns are **bold** and the adjectives in *italics* to help you.)

Today's **apology**, however *inadequate*, is aimed at righting *past* **wrongs**. It is also aimed at building a **bridge** between Indigenous and non-Indigenous Australians—a **bridge** based on a *real* **respect** rather than a *thinly veiled* **contempt**.

Work on words

Increasing your word power

When writing, it's good to think about ways to make your ideas clearer and more **concise**. Many writers often use the same small words when they are trying to describe something, such as *get*, *bad* and *good*. However, finding a **more descriptive** word will increase the power and **effectiveness** of your writing.

1 Look at the following phrases. Choose a word from the word bank that is a more **effective** and **concise** choice. The first one has been done for you.

distinctive	pseudonym	gamut	stalemate	vitality	alienate

a one of a kind distinctive

b vigorous health ________

c make an enemy ________

d deadlocked situation ________

e fictitious name ________

f a whole range ________

2 Choose a **more descriptive** word from the list to replace the **bold** word in each sentence. The first one has been done for you.

persuade	inferior	benevolent	congenial	noxious	propagate

a I hope I can **get** ___persuade___ my mum to let me go out on Saturday night.

b There are some very **good** ____________ people who donate their time to charities.

c Olivia is a very **nice** ____________ girl who gets on well with everyone.

d Word of mouth will **get** ____________ more business for our online business.

e It never pays to buy clothes of **bad** ____________ quality.

f There was an increasingly **bad** ____________ smell coming from the open sewer.

Kevin Rudd uses wordy language to **appeal** to our **emotions** and often repeats ideas so that we do not misunderstand his message. He also uses **everyday** and **colloquial** expressions and phrases so he does not alienate his audience. These create the effect of having a conversation with the audience, rather than of telling them what to do.

3 Look at the following examples from the *Sorry Day* speech and suggest several words to replace each phrase. The first one has been done for you.

a … whose lives were **ripped apart**

destroyed, ruined, wrecked or damaged

b There is nothing I can say today that can **take away** the pain

____

____

c Imagine the **crippling effect**

____

____

d Today's apology … is aimed at righting **past wrongs**

____

____

e It is also aimed at **building a bridge** between Indigenous and non-Indigenous Australians

____

____

f Unless … reconciliation is accompanied by an even greater substance, it is little more than **a clanging gong**

____

____

Spotlight on language

Rhetoric—the skill of speeches

Rhetoric is the art of communication—an art that aims to improve the skills of speakers who want to **inform**, **persuade** or **motivate** particular audiences in specific situations. A speech differs from a written text, such as an essay, in that listeners are unable to read what is being said and must rely only on what they hear. In addition, a speech delivered by a politician, such as the *Sorry Day* speech, may be broadcast over a variety of media including television, radio and the internet. As a result, speakers rely on a number of **key techniques** that allow them to communicate their ideas clearly and effectively.

These include:

- **emotive language**—this is language which is charged with emotion, such as *love*, *hate* and *fear*. Emotive language is deliberately designed to arouse the emotions. Speech makers use emotive language to create an emotional impact or response in their audience.

1 Look at the bold **emotive** words in the following sentences from the *Sorry Day* speech. Choose a word from the list that has the same meaning, but less emotional impact. You will see that this reduces the impact of the sentence. The first one has been done for you.

discomfort disagreeable enthusiastic discourtesy weakening

a We apologise for the hurt, the pain and **suffering** that we, the parliament, have caused you by the laws that previous parliaments have enacted. discomfort

b We apologise for the **indignity**, the degradation and the humiliation these laws embodied. ______

c ... within a decade to halve the **appalling** gap in infant mortality rates between Indigenous and non-Indigenous children. ______

d Imagine the **crippling** effect. Imagine how hard it would be to forgive. ______

e Australians are a **passionate** lot. We are also a very practical lot. ______

- **repetition**—the intended use of repetition adds emphasis and intensifies the style of the text. Through the use of repetition, key words or ideas are emphasised and made more memorable to the audience. As a rhetorical device, it is used to appeal to the emotions of the audience and encourage pathos in order to persuade and motivate.

2 Look at the following example from the *Sorry Day* speech. Highlight the **repeated words** and **ideas**. What is the key message being delivered to the audience?

To the stolen generations, I say the following: as Prime Minister of Australia, I am sorry. On behalf of the government of Australia, I am sorry. On behalf of the parliament of Australia, I am sorry. I offer you this apology without qualification. We apologise for the hurt, the pain and suffering that we, the parliament, have caused you by the laws that previous parliaments have enacted. We apologise for the indignity, the degradation and the humiliation these laws embodied.

______

______

* **metaphor**—in rhetoric, metaphor is primarily used to convey a new idea by linking it to an existing idea with which the audience is already familiar.

3 Look at the following example from the *Sorry Day* speech and then answer the questions.

Today's apology, however inadequate, is aimed at righting past wrongs. It is also aimed at **building a bridge** between Indigenous and non-Indigenous Australians—**a bridge** based on a real respect rather than a thinly veiled contempt. Our challenge for the future is to now **cross that bridge** and, in so doing, to embrace a new partnership between Indigenous and non-Indigenous Australians.

a A 'bridge' is a **metaphor** in that it stands for something else. What does it mean in the context of this speech?

b What kind of a 'bridge' is Kevin Rudd hoping to create?

c After introducing the **concept** of the 'bridge', Kevin Rudd then introduces a new concept of 'crossing the bridge'. What is this a **metaphor** for?

Extend your skills

Reflect on the topic: why is it important to offer an apology in order to encourage lasting and stable relationships?

Have your opinions on the relationship between Indigenous and non-Indigenous Australians changed after working through the chapter? If so, how?

UNIT EIGHT

Autobiography

Before you read

Looking at **headings**, **subheadings** and **introductions** before you read a text is a good **previewing technique**. It will help you understand the content and purpose of what you are about to read.

Read only the **title** and the **introduction**; then answer the following questions.

1 The writer tells us he is 'speaking from the grave'. What does this mean?

______

______

______

2 Tick (✓) the correct answer. Why does the writer want to 'speak from the grave'?

a because he will shortly be dead ______

b because he can speak honestly and without obstruction ______

c because he thinks being dead will increase his readership ______

3 Tick (✓) the correct answer. Look at the **headings**. What do you think the rest of the text will mainly be about?

a the future ______

b the present ______

c the past ______

Excerpts from the autobiography of Mark Twain

Excerpts from the autobiography of Mark Twain

Introduction

In this Autobiography I shall keep in mind the fact that I am speaking from the grave. I am literally speaking from the grave, because I shall be dead when the book issues from the press.

I speak from the grave rather than with my living tongue, for a good reason: I can speak thence freely. When a man is writing a book dealing with the privacies of his life—a book which is to be read while he is still alive—he shrinks from speaking his whole frank mind; all his attempts to do it fail, he recognizes that he is trying to do a thing which is wholly impossible to a human being.

EARLY FRAGMENTS 1870-1877

I will construct a text:

What a wee little part of a person's life are his acts and his words! His real life is led in his head, and is known to none but himself. All day long, and every day, the mill of his brain is grinding, and his *thoughts*, not those other things, are his history. His acts and his words are merely the visible, thin crust of his world, with its scattered snow summits and its vacant wastes of water—and they are so trifling a part of his bulk! a mere skin enveloping it. The mass of him is hidden—it and its volcanic fires that toss and boil, and never rest, night nor day. These are his life, and they are not written, and cannot be written. Every day would make a whole book of eighty thousand words—three hundred and sixty-five books a year. Biographies are but the clothes and buttons of the man—the biography of the man himself cannot be written.

WRITTEN ABOUT 1870—THE TENNESSEE LAND

The monster tract of land which our family own in Tennessee was purchased by my father a little over forty years ago. He bought the enormous area of seventy-five thousand acres at one purchase. The entire lot must have cost him somewhere in the neighbourhood of four hundred dollars. That was a good deal of money to pass over at one payment in those days—at least it was considered so away up there in the pineries and the 'Knobs' of the Cumberland Mountains of Fentress County, East Tennessee. When my father paid down that great sum, and turned and stood in the courthouse door of Jamestown, and looked abroad over his vast possessions, he said, "Whatever befalls me, my heirs are secure; I shall not live to see these acres turn to silver and gold, but my children will." Thus with the very kindest intentions in the world toward us, he laid the heavy curse of prospective wealth upon our shoulders. He went to his grave in the full belief that he had done us a kindness. It was a woeful mistake, but, fortunately, he never knew it.

Source: http://gutenberg.net.au/ebooks02/0200551

Test your understanding

1 Tick (✓) the correct answer. The autobiography extract is structured into THREE main sections. What tense order do these sections mainly follow?

- **a** present—past—past ______
- **b** future—past—present ______
- **c** present—present—past ______
- **d** present—future—present ______

2 Tick (✓) the correct answer. The author Mark Twain tells us that when a man is alive he 'shrinks from speaking his whole frank mind.' What does this mean?

- **a** speaks freely and openly about his thoughts and feelings ______
- **b** physically leaves a situation where he is asked to give an opinion ______
- **c** counsels others on being honest and open ______
- **d** is fearful talking about what he really thinks and feels ______

3 What does the author mean when he describes acts and words of a person's life as *wee*? Circle the THREE best answers.

- **a** insignificant
- **b** microscopic
- **c** minor
- **d** short
- **e** compact
- **f** small
- **g** early

4 Tick (✓) the correct answer. What is the line 'The mill of his brain is grinding' (under 'I will construct a text') an example of?

- **a** metaphor ______
- **b** simile ______

c assonance ______

d hyperbole ______

5 Tick (✓) the correct answer. What does 'The mill of his brain is grinding …' reveal about what the man's brain is actually doing?

a thinking of a pepper grinder ______

b working, in action, thinking ______

c under pressure ______

d slowing down ______

6 Tick (✓) the correct answer. What is the overall purpose of the second section of the extract (under the subheading, 'I will construct a text')?

a to discuss the trivialities of life and how 'wee' our actions actually are ______

b to attempt to link ideas about personality to images of the natural environment ______

c to provide reasons why writing biographies is so challenging ______

d to explain that we are more our thoughts and feelings, rather than our actions and words ______

7 Tick (✓) the correct answer. In the same section the author writes 'These are his life'. What does the author mean?

a his secret lives ______

b his thoughts ______

c his travel experiences ______

d his history ______

8 Tick (✓) the correct answer. What does 'Biographies are but the clothes and buttons of the man' say about the nature of biographies?

a a man needs a biography as much as he needs clothes with buttons ______

b a biography does not begin with a person's birth ______

c biographies focus on the everyday events of a person's life ______

d biographies rarely express a person's inner thoughts ______

9 Tick (✓) the correct answer. After reading the final paragraph, what motivated Twain's father to purchase a 'monster tract of land'?

a he wanted to become a wealthy land owner ______

b he wanted to protect his children's financial future and success ______

c he wanted the act to be remembered as a kindness ______

d the land was cheap and didn't cost him much to purchase ______

10 Tick (✓) the correct answer. We can't tell for sure from the text but what do you think was the 'woeful mistake' Twain's father made?

a he sold the land before he died ______

b the land became worthless and was a poor investment ______

c his generosity did not result in the family's happiness or good fortune ______

d he died before he saw the land result in success for his family and heirs ______

11 Tick (✓) the correct answer. What is the tone of this text?

a reflective and informative ______

b argumentative and nostalgic ______

c despairing and emotional ______

d conversational and instructional ______

Boost your reading skills

Understanding point of view

Narrative writing is always told from someone's **point of view**. This point of view is the perspective from which characters and events are presented by the **narrator** or '**voice**' of the narrative. The point of view in a story reveals the **relationship** between the narrator and the story, including the characters in it. The point of view chosen can have a strong effect on the reader.

There are three main points of view used by writers:

- **first person narrative**—the main character tells his or her own story. The narrator refers to him- or herself by using the pronouns *I*, *me* or *mine*, or the plurals *we* and *our*.
- **third-person omniscient**—the narrator is all-seeing, all-knowing and all thoughts are revealed. The author enters each character's minds as an observer of the whole story. The story is told in the third person (*he*, *she*, *it* or *they*).
- **third-person limited**—the story is told in the third person, but as seen through the eyes of one character only. The author only enters the mind of one character, not all of them. The characters reveal themselves through what they say about themselves and others, and through their actions.

1 Answer the following questions to review your knowledge of **point-of-view**. Answer each question using either the **first person**, **third-person omniscient** or **third-person limited**.

a If you are a narrator who wants to appear in the story, which **narrative point-of-view** would you choose?

____

____

b If you are the narrator, and you are outside the story and able to look into the mind of only one character, which narrative point-of-view are you using?

____

____

c Which point of view should you use in order to be able to read the minds of all characters?

____

____

d If a narrator is obviously in favour of the opinions of one particular character, which point of view is the narrator most likely using?

____

____

2 Mark Twain uses a variety of points of view depending on his purpose. For each of the following examples from the extract, decide if they use the **first person**, **third-person omniscient** or **third-person limited**.

a I shall keep in mind that I am speaking from the grave

____

b When a man is writing a book dealing with the privacies of his life …

____

c His real life is led in his head

____

d was purchased by my father a little over forty years ago

____

e What a wee little part of a person's life are his acts and his words!

____

3 The following information focuses on Twain's use of **narrative view**. Fill in the gaps from the list to show your understanding.

omniscient	experiences	shared	two	personalises

Twain uses ______________ main narrative points of views—first person and third-person ______________. He uses the first person when talking about his real life experiences. First-person narrative ______________ the experience and provides the 'voice' of the narrator. It also focuses the reader on the writer's life and ______________.

Twain shifts to the third-person omniscient point-of-view when talking about the wider experience of life and writing. In doing so, Twain creates a sense of a ______________ experience and is able to speak for 'all' people.

Work on words

Words derived from Greek

Etymology is known as the study of word origins and involves tracing word development throughout history. Studying word origins will help you gain a better understanding of language in general.

Having some understanding of the meaning of a Greek **root**, **prefix** or **suffix** will help you make connections between other similar sounding words that exist in English. It may even help you interpret the meanings of words you do not know the meaning of.

For example: knowing that the Greek prefix *tele* means 'far' or 'far off' will help you quickly understand the meanings of words such as *telescope*, *television*, *telephone* and *telepathy*.

1 The Greek word *auto* means 'self'. Can you think of any other words in English that contain the prefix *auto*?

____

____

2 The Greek prefix *crypto* means 'hide'.

Match the following words with the prefix *crypto* to their correct meaning by drawing a line between them. The first one has been done for you.

cryptic	put into code/expressed in code
encrypted	a hidden vault
cryptology	the text part of a message that is in coded form
crypt	deliberately mysterious with a hidden meaning
crypto text	the study of encoding and decoding plain messages

3 Each set of words on the right below share a Greek prefix. Match each set to the meaning of the prefix on the left.

Definitions	Prefix examples
a wheel, circle	democracy, epidemic, demographic
b through, across	hydraulics, hydrant, hydrophobia
c people	monoplane, monotone
d race, nation	cyclone, cycle, bicycle
e blood	pneumatic, pneumonia
f water	geography, geometry
g one, alone	pyromaniac, pyrotechnics
h air, breath	diameter, dialogue
i fire	haemorrhage, anaemia
j earth	ethnic, ethnology

Spotlight on language

Extended metaphors

Figurative language includes special forms that writers use to help readers make a strong connection to their words. Figurative language includes **similes**, **metaphors**, **personification** and **hyperbole**.

1 Review your knowledge of **figurative language** by reading the following examples from the work of another author, Edgar Allen Poe. Identify each as **simile**, **metaphor**, **personification** or **hyperbole**.

- **a** The breeze—the breath of God—is still ______________________
- **b** A single dim ray, like the thread of the spider, shot from out the crevice ______________________
- **c** Yes, he was stone, stone dead ______________________
- **d** Death has reared himself a throne/In a strange city lying alone ______________________
- **e** All that we see or seem/Is but a dream within a dream ______________________
- **f** Above all was the sense of hearing acute. I heard all things in the heaven and in the earth ______________________

A **metaphor** is one kind of figurative language as it makes a direct **comparison** between two unlike things. A metaphor that governs throughout a poem is called an extended metaphor. Extended metaphors allow writers to draw a larger comparison between two things or ideas. They highlight a comparison in a more **vivid** and **powerful** way than simple metaphors or similes.

2 In the following example, Shakespeare is comparing the world to a stage. Underline all the references to the stage that he uses to **extend** the **metaphor**.

All the world's a stage, and all the men and women merely players,
They have their exits and their entrances
And one man in his time plays many parts. (*As You Like It*)

3 Mark Twain uses **extended metaphor** relating to the natural world in order to convey a sense of how difficult it is to write down the truth about people in biographies. Look at the following examples from the autobiography extract and then answer the questions.

His acts and his words are merely the visible, thin crust of his world, with its scattered snow summits and its vacant wastes of water …

- **a** What does Twain compare a man's 'acts and words' to?

  ____

- **b** In using an **extended metaphor** of the physical world, Twain creates an image of the man's acts and words being the 'crust'. What are his thoughts and feelings represented as being?

  ____

4 Tick (✓) the correct answer. What does this **extended metaphor** show about a man's personality?

- **a** a man's personality is more complex than it appears on the outside, or 'crust' ______
- **b** a man's personality is rugged and dangerous like the physical world ______
- **c** a man's personality is shallow and lacks depth ______
- **d** a man's personality is private and should not be explored or revealed ______

5 How is someone feeling if their inner self, as Twain says, is 'tossing and boiling' and 'never resting'? Write three adjectives that could explain these ideas.

Extend your skills

Have a go at writing about your own life experience in an **autobiographical** style. Choose one of the following topics or events as a basis for writing about your own experiences, or choose another event of your own.

worst memory	family	friends	best memory	pets	hobbies	school experiences

Event chosen:

1 Now write about your event and zoom in by using the following guidelines.

a Your event should focus on a 'moment in time'. What 'moment in time' are you focusing on?

b Tell the outside story: what was happening in your world when the event occurred?

c Tell the inside story—what were you thinking and feeling during the event?

d Use dialogue (conversation) to create immediacy and realism about your event.

e What are some details that only you, as the writer, knows about what happened?

2 Now bring your ideas together and create two or three paragraphs about your experience. Use the following language guidelines to improve the power and effect of your autobiography extract.

- Use **vivid** and **powerful words**—adjectives, strong verbs, specific nouns and adverbs.
- Use **poetic devices**—simile, onomatopoeia, metaphor and alliteration.
- Use a **variety** of **sentence lengths** and **sentence types**—simple, compound, complex and compound-complex.
- Use different **sentence beginnings** to add variety to your expression.
- Use different **sentence types**—statements, exclamations, questions and commands.

UNIT NINE

Environmental article

Before you read

1 Tick (✓) the correct answer. Read the **headline** and first **subheadline** only. What do you think the article will tell you about?

- a american computers ______
- b mistakes made in computer disposal ______
- c the number of computers being disposed ______

2 Now quickly skim the remaining bolded subheadings in the article. Does doing this confirm or change the choice you made in question 1?

____

3 What do you and your family do with your old computers, computer parts or mobile phones?

____

____

4 Do you think it's important to recycle old computers and electronic waste? Why/Why not?

____

____

____

Computer recycling

Importance of Computer Recycling

Peter Wendt

Technology Articles | December, 2013

Each year, Americans dispose of hundreds of millions of computer product units. Most of that e-waste joins our already teeming landfill or goes to outside incinerators.

E-Wasted

1 E-waste, including computer waste, is causing significant health and environmental concerns in the developing world. Each year, Americans dispose of hundreds of millions of computer product units. Most of that e-waste joins our already teeming landfill or goes to outside incinerators. Recently, e-waste is increasingly shipped to Asia. Only a portion of the items discarded, about 40 million units, is recycled. Not only is this a mammoth waste of crude materials, it is a significant danger to our environment. Here in the USA, Environmental Protection Agency officials agree that the environmental dangers of discarded computer equipment cannot be overstated. CRTs alone contain lead, cadmium, mercury, beryllium and other hazardous materials. In addition to the actively discarded items, the EPA estimates that nearly 3/4s of the computers sold in the US are gathering dust in home storage spaces. This is landfill waiting to happen.

What is being e-wasted?

2 Aside from the issue of environmental impact, this means that valuable materials are simply being thrown away. Some of the printed circuit boards contain precious metals such as silver,

gold, and platinum. They also contain base metals like iron and copper. There is not yet a satisfying method of completely recycling these circuit boards, though there are several possibilities on the horizon.

What else is wasted?

3 When there is poor use made of existing computer goods, further manufacturing is promoted. The cheap price of new units makes upgrading prohibitive to many people. This encourages the creation of waste from the production of the new units, as well as the packaging discards from shipping them. The old computer is moved to the basement. The new one is purchased to be put in its place. In developing countries, however, what the US might consider an outmoded computer system might be seen as a miraculous gift. Also, even in the US, many schools are badly in need of computer equipment. Refurbishing old systems and sending them along to where they are still needed is a significant method of recycling.

The future of recycling:

4 Public recycling of electronics has been a thorny issue, since e-waste presents a danger to workers in local recycling centres. This is where business can come into play. There are new recycling methods being developed every day. There are large electronic recyclers that specialise in the safe dismantling and recycling of computer equipment. Some companies reduce the units to their constituent elements like metal, glass and plastic. This provides much cheaper raw materials for manufacturing.

The only limits to this are the limits of the human imagination. Creative thinking is all that is needed to expand the future possibilities for computer recycling.

Source: Free Articles from ArticlesFactory.com http://www.articlesfactory.com/articles/technology/importance-of-computer-recycling.html

Test your understanding

1 Tick (✓) the correct answer. What is e-waste?

- **a** energy waste ______
- **b** environmental waste ______
- **c** electronic waste ______
- **d** exported waste ______

2 Tick (✓) the correct answer. What does the word 'teeming' (paragraph 1) mean?

- **a** joining ______
- **b** boiling or simmering ______
- **c** jam packed, crowded ______
- **d** busy, occupied ______

3 Tick (✓) the correct answer. What does 'On the horizon' also mean?

- **a** on top of things ______
- **b** out to sea ______
- **c** in the distance ______
- **d** in the future ______

4 According to the article, why do most people buy a new computer rather than upgrade their existing one?

____

____

5 The following terms are from the article and relate to the topic. Look at the context of the word to help you match them to their correct meaning.

a *actively discarded* (paragraph 1)	basic components
b *teeming landfill* (introduction)	cathode ray tube
c *crude materials* (paragraph 1)	deliberately thrown away
d *CRT* (paragraph 1)	restoring or overhauling units
e *refurbishing old systems* (paragraph 3)	basic or simple resources
f *constituent elements* (paragraph 4)	overflowing tip or rubbish dump

6 Tick (✓) the correct answer. What does the article suggest should be done with most old computer units?

a refurbish, then ship to Asia ______

b send to landfill or incineration ______

c dismantle safely then recycle ______

d give to US schools ______

7 Using your own words, explain the following sentence.
In developing countries, however, what the US might consider an outmoded computer system might be seen as a miraculous gift.

____

____

____

____

8 Tick (✓) the correct answer. What is the purpose of the article?

a to entertain and inform ______

b to inform and persuade ______

c to persuade and describe ______

d to recount and explain ______

9 Which information in the article was most surprising to you?

____

____

____

____

10 The article is written about an American context and does not relate directly to Australia. In what ways do you think it can be considered still relevant to an Australian audience?

____

____

____

____

Boost your reading skills

Scanning for specific information

Scanning is a reading skill used to locate **specific information** quickly, such as dates, numbers, examples and definitions. Scanning involves a method of quickly searching what you are reading in order to locate specific pieces of information. When scanning you don't start from the beginning and read to the end. Instead, you jump around within the text, trying to locate the information you require. You probably already scan the internet or dictionaries, but scanning techniques can also be useful when researching or reading text books.

Using the article *Importance of Computer Recycling*, follow these steps for scanning.

- Look for **key words** or words that are **repeated**.

1 Which FOUR words are **repeated** in the first paragraph of the article?

____

2 Do you agree that these words are the **key words** for the whole article? Why/Why not?

____

- Look for **highlighted** words (e.g. words in **bold** or *italic*).

3 Which sections of the article are written in **bold**? Why?

____

- Look for **numbers** (e.g. dates, statistics, figures or numbers).

4 In the first paragraph, **scan** for TWO examples of statistical information.

____

- Look for **examples**.

5 In paragraph 1, **scan** for hazardous elements contained in CRTs.

____

____

6 In paragraph 2, **scan** for examples of precious metals.

____

____

7 In paragraph 4, **scan** for examples of computer constituent elements.

____

____

Scanning and the internet

It is very likely that you **scan** when you surf the **internet**. People rarely read web pages word by word; instead, they are more likely to scan the page, identifying individual words and ideas.

As a result, web pages are created using **scannable text** that features:

- highlighted **key words** that allow **main ideas** and **concepts** to stand out
- well-chosen **subheadings** that help **identify** the **main idea** of the paragraph
- **bulleted lists** so that information is **clearly organised** and '**chunked**'
- one **main idea** per paragraph
- smaller **word count** per page than other texts, such as a textbook.

8 Find a web page and assess it using the above criteria. How '**scannable**' is the website you are viewing based on its organisation?

____

____

____

____

____

____

Work on words

Adverbs and adjectives

Adverbs modify—or add to the meaning of—verbs, adjectives or other adverbs. Adverbs tell **how**, **when** and **where** something is done and the **degree** to which the activity takes place. They can show:

- **time** (e.g. he will go **soon**)
- **place** (e.g. she goes **there**)
- **manner** (e.g. they shouted **noisily**)
- **number** (e.g. she tried **once**)
- **degree** (e.g. it had **nearly** begun).

1 Using the examples above as a guide, write what kind of **adverb** each underlined word is—**time**, **place**, **manner**, **number** or **degree**. The first one has been done for you.

a I'm happy to set up the computer <u>anywhere</u> that suits you. ___place___

b The computer worked <u>efficiently</u> before then blowing a fuse. ______________

c I restarted the system <u>once</u> before calling a technician. ______________

d She felt tired <u>enough</u> to rest, but had to continue researching online. ______________

e Telemarketers <u>regularly</u> call during dinner, much to my irritation. ______________

f I <u>already</u> knew how to fix the problem but had to wait to update my computer. ______________

2 This is more challenging: decide which kind of **adverb** each underlined word is. Ask yourself **how**, **when**, **where** or to what **degree**. The first one has been done for you.

a Most of that e-waste joins our already teeming landfill or goes to outside incinerators. time

b In addition to the actively discarded items, the EPA estimates that nearly three quarters of the computers sold in the US are gathering dust in home storage spaces. ____________

c Aside from the issue of environmental impact, this poor utilisation of these items means that valuable materials are being simply thrown away. ____________

d There is not yet a satisfying method of completely recycling these circuit boards, though there are several possibilities on the horizon. ____________

e When there is poor use made of existing computer goods, further manufacturing is promoted. ____________

f Also, even in the US, many schools are badly in need of computer equipment. ____________

g This provides much cheaper raw materials for manufacturing. ____________

People sometimes get **adverbs** and **adjectives** confused when constructing sentences. Don't forget that adverbs modify **verbs** (*doing* or *action* words), while adjectives are used to modify **nouns** (*people, places* or *things*).

3 Write the correct choice of word in these sentences. The first one has been done for you.

a I didn't think I felt (good/well) well after sitting in front of the computer for three hours.

b Recycling your old computer will (real/really) ________ help others in need.

c The business did not dispose of their old systems (proper/properly) ________ so they were fined.

d It felt (good/well) ________ to know that I helped the environment by taking the time to recycle.

e New technology emerges fairly (quick/quickly) ________ and people like to keep up.

f Recycling (bad/badly) ________ has a wider impact on society and the environment.

g It is better to take the time to manage old hardware effectively (then/than) ________ to act in haste.

Spotlight on language

Syntax

Syntax is how sentences are structured. Sentences have to follow certain rules in order to make sense. It's not possible to throw just any words together to make a sentence. Native speakers learn the syntax of their language as small children and mostly use it correctly when speaking. Those who learn a second language have to study it more formally.

Being aware of syntax is helpful for any student when reading and writing complex texts. So, too, is the learning of **metalanguage**—the language that describes language.

The following terms are examples of metalanguage that describe syntax and English grammar: subject, verb and predicate

All sentences are about someone or something. This is called the **subject** of the sentence. The **verb** is the 'doing' or action word and the **predicate** is the remaining information (including the verb).

For example: People swim in pools.

The verb is *swim*.

To find the subject, ask *who* or *what* before the verb: the answer is *people*.

The remaining information after the subject is the predicate (include the verb: *swim in pools*).

1 Underline the **subjects** in the following sentences and circle the **verbs**. Note that the subject is often, but not always, the first thing in the sentence. The first one has been done for you.

- **a** Cate often works on her computer in the evenings.
- **b** My mother and I both have the same phone.
- **c** Many parts of the telecommunications system were destroyed by the storm.
- **d** The unused classroom near the library is going to be redeveloped into a computer room.
- **e** Standing on the roof on the top of the house was a large aerial and satellite dish.
- **f** During holidays we often text about lunch.
- **g** Lying on the beach with a good kindle book is my favourite thing to do.

2 Analyse the following sentences from the *Importance of Computer Recycling* article. Underline the **subjects**, circle the **verbs** and put a line through the **predicate**. The first one has been done for you.

- **a** This provides ~~much cheaper raw materials~~ for manufacturing.
- **b** The only limits to this are the limits of the human imagination.
- **c** Creative thinking is all that is needed to expand the future possibilities for computer recycling.
- **d** This is landfill waiting to happen
- **e** Some of the printed circuit boards contain precious metals such as silver, gold, and platinum.
- **f** They also contain base metals like iron and copper.

Extend your skills

Create a short advertisement for an e-waste company. In your advertisement you should:

- create a business name
- create a business logo (a small visual image that represents the ideals of a business)
- provide a definition of e-waste
- provide a list of items to recycle
- provide persuasive reasons for recycling.

UNIT TEN

Poems

Before you read

It is always easier to understand what you are reading if you have some **background knowledge** and **experience** of the topic. Activating this knowledge and experience helps you make connections between new and known information.

1 The poem you are about to read was written in Australia in 1900. In what way does this influence your opinion about what you are going to read?

2 Have you heard of Henry Lawson? Note down anything you know about him.

My Literary Friend by Henry Lawson from *Verses Popular and Humorous* (1900)

Once I wrote a little poem which I thought was very fine,
And I showed the printer's copy to a critic friend of mine,
First he praised the thing a little, then he found a little fault;
'The ideas are good,' he muttered, 'but the rhythm seems to halt.'

So I straighten'd up the rhythm where he marked it with his pen,
And I copied it and showed it to my clever friend again.
'You've improved the metre greatly, but the rhymes are bad,' he said,
As he read it slowly, scratching surplus wisdom from his head.

So I worked as he suggested (I believe in taking time),
And I burnt the 'midnight taper' while I straightened up the rhyme.
'It is better now,' he muttered, 'you go on and you'll succeed,
'It has got a ring about it—the ideas are what you need.'

So I worked for hours upon it (I go on when I commence),
And I kept in view the rhythm and the jingle and the sense,
And I copied it and took it to my solemn friend once more—
It reminded him of something he had somewhere read before.

♦ ♦ ♦

Now the people say I'd never put such horrors into print
If I wasn't too conceited to accept a friendly hint,
And my dearest friends are certain that I'd profit in the end
If I'd always show my copy to a literary friend.

Source: http://gutenberg.net.au/ebooks06/0607601h.html#s21

Test your understanding

1 Tick (✓) the correct answer. Who is the 'literary friend'?

- **a** the poet, Henry Lawson ______
- **b** a friend of Lawson's ______
- **c** an invented character—a literary critic ______
- **d** an invented character—a poet ______

2 Tick (✓) the correct answer. When the 'friend' says that the ideas are 'good' he is most likely saying that they are

- **a** satisfying. ______
- **b** original. ______
- **c** fun. ______
- **d** well behaved. ______

3 Tick (✓) the correct answer. The poet character says he 'straighten'd up the rhythm' because

- **a** none of the poem rhymed properly. ______
- **b** the poet had written outside the lines on the paper the critic read from. ______
- **c** it stopped suddenly and interrupted the beat of the poem. ______
- **d** the critic didn't like it. ______

4 Tick (✓) the correct answer. The poet character is told 'You've improved the metre greatly'. Based on what is written in the first two verses of the poem, what do you think 'metre' refers to?

- **a** a rhythm of syllables that creates an internal beat to the poem as it is read ______
- **b** the length of each line in the poem ______
- **c** the number of lines in a stanza, or verse, within a poem ______
- **d** the effect created when lines rhyme in poetry ______

5 Using your own words, explain what 'scratching surplus wisdom' reveals about what the critic is actually doing? What does it say about the poet character's opinion of him?

____

____

____

7 Tick (✓) the correct answer. 'I believe in taking time' is an example of

a an aside by the character. ______

b a quote from the poem. ______

c the critic's voice. ______

d a soliloquy by a character in the poem. ______

8 Tick (✓) the correct answer. What does it mean to 'burn the midnight taper'?

a to burn unwanted paper in a bin ______

b to work long and hard at night ______

c to light a candle at night to work by ______

d to sleep ______

9 Tick (✓) the correct answer. Something that has 'a ring about it' means

a an idea that makes you remember something else. ______

b a line that has effect of hearing bells as you read it. ______

c an idea with a certain charm, that has something memorable about it. ______

d a line that the critic has circled as he is reviewing the persona's work. ______

10 Tick (✓) the correct answer. The poet considers 'rhythm', 'jingle' and 'sense' in his poem. This means he is focused on

a the beat, sound and ideas in the poem. ______

b the beat and advertising potential of the poem. ______

c the sound, ideas and logic of the poem. ______

d whether the poem could be put to music or not. ______

11 Tick (✓) the correct answer. After all the work the poet does revising his work, the critic states 'It reminded him of something he had read somewhere before'. The effect of this is

a critical—the poet is criticising the critic. ______

b humorous—despite all the persona's work, the poem has lost its originality. ______

c frustrating—the persona will be annoyed with the result. ______

d revealing—it reveals the critic's final criticism of the poem. ______

12 Tick (✓) the correct answer. The feeling of the final stanza is

a reflective and self-critical. ______

b argumentative and nostalgic. ______

c despairing and emotional. ______

d conversational and instructional. ______

Boost your reading skills

Reading poetry

Reading a **poem** isn't just about being able to pronounce the words or understand individual definitions—it requires that you obtain an overall sense of what the poet is really trying to **communicate** or say. Poems are generally short and more intense, with less of a conventional story to follow, and you may need to 'read between the lines' in order to understand it's **overall purpose** and **message**.

The following list of poetic features will help you 'read' a poem. These questions can be answered when reading any poem; however, you should answer them now in consideration of Henry Lawson's *My Literary Friend*.

- **Title**—what hints or clues does the title of the poem give you? Does the title point towards potential themes of the poem? Is it an effective title?

- **Point of view**—whose point of view is represented in the poem? (e.g. Who is talking? Who are they talking to?)

- **Theme**—what is the main idea or theme of the poem? If someone asked you, 'What's this poem about?' how would you respond?

* **Poet's purpose**—why do you think the poet wrote the poem?

* How does the poem **sound**? Read the poem aloud: does it move quickly or slowly? Does it sound awkward in sections or does it have an even flow? Do certain words stick out more than others? If the poem sounds odd in places, the poet may be highlighting an important idea.

* **Word pictures**—what do you 'see' in your mind as you read the poem? Has the poet used identifiable techniques such as personification, similes or metaphors to convey his ideas?

Work on words

Formal and informal register

Poets may choose to use **formal** or **informal register** in their poems. A poem that uses everyday, informal language can be just as powerful as a poem that uses sophisticated, formal language.

* **Formal register**—the poet chooses words or phrases that appear more elegant or extravagant. Often formal register will contain words that are **polysyllabic** (that contain many syllables).
  For example: conceited
* **Informal register**—the poet chooses words or phrases that are considered ordinary and for everyday usage. These may be words and phrases that are **slang** or **colloquial** expressions. **Contractions** are also often used in poetry and reflect the language of conversation.
  For example: straighten'd a ring about it

Australia defined its 'bush' identity during the 1890s, and Henry Lawson's work helped create a particular image of Australia that is still held today. His characters reflect his experiences of the world and feature 'real' people who are down on their luck, traveling workers and 'bush larrikins' (rough and rowdy country 'characters'). The **informal**, **colloquial** and **slang** language choices he made appealed to his audience of the period and reinforced what it meant to be Australian.

1 Look at Henry Lawson's poem. List some examples of **formal** and **informal language** you find.

____

____

2 The following is a list of lines and phrases that can be found in Henry Lawson's poems. Match the underlined **informal term** in each example to its modern definition on the right.

a	Than e'er it ran before	unemployed, unoccupied, lazy
b	For the commonwealth of idlers	ever
c	'Twas Mulga Bill, from Eaglehawk, that caught the cycling craze	remote from major populations
d	That would tide him o'er the morrow	ought to
e	Where the scrubs and plains are wide	It was
f	And the time had come, as the shearer knew, to carry his swag Out Back	low, thick bush
g	magpie up in the scrub, and yer oughter be able to catch it.	over

Spotlight on language

Rhythm and rhyme

Rhyme is the use of words with identical final sounds and is one of the more obvious poetic techniques. Rhyme can be an important part of poetry, and there are many different types of rhyme. Poets may rhyme at the beginning or end of each line of poetry, or within the line itself.

There are two main kinds of rhyme:

- **full** or **exact rhymes**—the major final sounds are identical (e.g. *time* and *prime*)
- **near** or **inexact rhymes**—words that rhyme because they have similar, but not identical, sounds (e.g. *thumb* and *gun*)

1 Rhyme is determined by **sound**, not **spelling**, so don't be fooled. Tick (✓) which of these two pairs of words rhyme.

a puff/enough ______

b through/though ______

2 Read the following poetic examples. Circle the **exact** rhymes and underline the **inexact** ones.

a I saw a fairy in the wood/He drew his sword while I just stood

b In mist or cloud, on mast or shroud

c Whiles all the night through fog-smoke white

d Then be not coy, but use your time/And while ye may, go marry/For having lost but one your prime

e Silver bells/What a world of merriment their melody foretells!

f The whiskey on your breath/Could make a small boy dizzy/But I hung on like death: Such waltzing was not easy

g Once upon a midnight dreary, while I pondered, weak and weary
Over many a quaint and curious volume of forgotten lore—
While I nodded, nearly napping, suddenly there came a tapping,
As of someone gently rapping, rapping at my chamber door—
"'Tis some visitor," I muttered, "tapping at my chamber door—
Only this and nothing more."

A **rhyme scheme** is a way of describing the pattern of **end** rhymes in a poem. Each new sound at the end of a line is assigned a letter, beginning with A, then B, and so on. If an end sound repeats the end sound of an earlier line, it gets the same letter as the earlier line.

For example: Roses are red (red gets **A** as its description)
Violets are blue (blue gets **B** because it does not rhyme with red)
Sugar is sweet (sweet gets **C** because it doesn't rhyme with red or blue)
And so are you! (you gets **B** because it rhymes with blue)
So the end rhyme scheme is: **A**, **B**, **C**, **B**.

3 Mark the following two examples to indicate their end **rhyme scheme**.

a From *Jabberwocky*

'Twas brillig, and the slithy toves
Did gyre and gimble in the wabe;
All mimsy were the borogroves,
And the mome raths outgrabe. ____________________

b *Sonnet 18* by William Shakespeare

Shall I compare thee to a summer's day?
Thou art more lovely and more temperate:
Rough winds do shake the darling buds of May,
And summer's lease hath all too short a date:

Sometime too hot the eye of heaven shines,
And often is his gold complexion dimm'd;
And every fair from fair sometime declines,
By chance, or nature's changing course untrimm'd;

But thy eternal summer shall not fade,
Nor lose possession of that fair thou ow'st,
Nor shall death brag thou wander'st in his shade,
When in eternal lines to time thou grow'st;

So long as men can breathe, or eyes can see,
So long lives this, and this gives life to thee. ______________

4 Identify the **rhyming scheme** used by Lawson in *My Literary Friend.* ______________

5 Complete the following sentences using the list below. The paragraph will help you understand the **effect** of Lawson's choice of **rhyme scheme**.

predictable	variation	simple	deliberately	humorous

In many ______________ poems, the final words in successive lines often rhyme. You may have noticed this in simple poems like nursery rhymes. Typically, this style of rhyming can become ______________ and fairly boring, and poets who choose to rhyme usually add greater ______________. Henry Lawson's use of a simple rhyme scheme works well, however. He has ______________ chosen this simple rhyming scheme as it enhances the light-hearted and ______________ effect of the poem.

Extend your skills

Research another Henry Lawson poem. Locate information about the context in which the poem is written and also its purpose—why did he write it? Consider the emotions created by specific words, images, and the storyline. What techniques did the poet use to communicate his ideas?

UNIT ELEVEN

Essays

Before you read

The **first paragraph** of any text is important as it provides key information about the **content**, **purpose** and **type** of **text** you are about to read. This sets up your expectations about the remainder of the text and makes it easier for you to read and understand it. Looking at an essay as a reader will help you when writing your own essays.

1 Read only the **first line** of paragraph one—choose five **key words** from the opening sentence of the essay. Write them here.

____

____

2 Based on your word choices, what do you think the essay will be about?

____

____

3 Tick (✓) the correct answer. Read the rest of the first paragraph. What do you think the essay will mostly focus on?

a Shakespeare's use of language ______

b Shakespeare's influence on our language ______

c the differences between Shakespeare's language and modern English ______

d Shakespeare's influence on spoken English ______

e Shakespeare's influence on written English ______

4 Now underline the sentence in the first paragraph which tells you this.

Shakespeare and language

1 Although the English language has been in a constant state of transition, William Shakespeare's work has continued to influence theatre, literature, present-day movies as well as the language we use daily. With Shakespeare's creation of commonly used expressions, his establishment of new words, and his use of punctuation, he was able to affect language in a way that was unprecedented. In examples of our everyday speech, and in his plays and poetry that have survived, Shakespeare's influence is evident.

2 Shakespeare's flair for moulding the English language into the powerful written word has ensured his lasting influence on our everyday language. Hundreds of clichés that are used daily by English speakers were invented by Shakespeare. Not many people are aware, but well-known expressions such as 'The course of true love never did run smooth' (*A Midsummer Night's Dream*) or 'To be, or not to be, that is the question' (*Hamlet*) can both be attributed to Shakespeare.

3 In addition, Shakespeare even took the liberty of inventing over one thousand frequently used words and expressions. Many of Shakespeare's original phrases are still used in conversation and language today. Some examples include 'seen better days', 'fashionable', 'newfangled', and 'uncomfortable'. Shakespeare's effect

on vocabulary is rather amazing when considering how much language has changed since his lifetime. Although a number of writers have used the English language to their advantage, no writer has had the influence that Shakespeare has.

4 Shakespeare's use of punctuation was also distinctive. Shakespeare used punctuation for a reason, and his punctuation, like his word and spelling choice, are clues to the way a piece should be performed. Punctuation is required to signal how each line should be delivered. It also forces the reader to pause and slows down the pace of the text. Consequently, lines without punctuation naturally seem to gather speed and emotional purpose. When reading aloud a speech written in verse, it is common to pause at the end of each line. Conversely, it is not necessary to do this unless the punctuation, such as a full stop, specifically requires this to occur. The movement of the sense of the idea into the next line allows the correct rhythm of the speech to be revealed. When analysing a Shakespearean script, stop and consider how punctuation is used.

5 In conclusion, despite Shakespeare's work being in constant use, he is not often given credit for his profound impact on the English language. He took the language of his time, altered it, shaped it, and revealed it through his eloquent and dramatic plays and sonnets. Shakespeare's impact on the English language may never be repeated; however we will always have the benefit of his insightful and powerful work.

Test your understanding

1 In the opening paragraph the word 'transition' appears. Re-read the opening sentence and then circle the three best synonyms (similar words) from the list.

change correction development compression progression reorganisation

2 Tick (✓) the correct answer. What is the purpose of the essay?

a to provide an entertaining insight into Shakespeare's life ______
b to inform and persuade about Shakespeare's great influence ______
c to compare the influence of various writers on the English language ______
d to influence people to read his plays and sonnets ______

3 Tick (✓) the correct answer. What is the overall main idea of the first paragraph?

a Shakespeare invented new words and phrases. ______
b Shakespeare influenced the way we speak. ______
c Shakespeare affected and influenced the English language. ______
d Shakespeare encouraged people to read more. ______

4 Tick (✓) the correct answer. Looking at the sentence, 'Shakespeare's talent for moulding the English language' (paragraph 2), which word could best replace 'moulding'?

a configuring ______
b manufacturing ______
c shaping ______
d controlling ______

5 Tick (✓) the correct answer. What does the line 'Consequently, lines without punctuation naturally seem to gather speed and emotional purpose' (paragraph 4) mean?

- **a** Punctuation increases the reader's emotional response to what they are reading. ______
- **b** Lines with no punctuation increase the pace and feeling of what is being read. ______
- **c** No punctuation adds naturalness and realism to Shakespeare's work. ______
- **d** Shakespeare preferred to use as little punctuation as possible. ______

6 Tick (✓) the correct answer. What is the meaning of the line 'The movement of the sense of the idea into the next line allows the correct rhythm of the speech to be revealed' (paragraph 4)?

- **a** The story is improved when ideas carry over onto other lines. ______
- **b** Not all ideas are revealed on one line, but need to be continued on to the next line. ______
- **c** Rhythm and speech are important features of Shakespearean language. ______
- **d** Reading into the next line without pausing creates a sense of natural speech. ______

7 Look back at the text for the following words and underline the best definition of each one. You may need to use a dictionary if the meanings are not made clear in the essay.

a *unprecedented* (paragraph 1):	not ever done before	the best ever	the most long lasting
b *liberty* (paragraph 3):	opportunity	skilfulness	responsibility
c *revealed* (paragraph 4):	unrestricted	exposed	hidden
d *articulate* (paragraph 5):	lucid	vivid	clear
e *profound* (paragraph 5):	intense	thoughtful	knowledgeable
f *eloquent* (paragraph 5):	well expressed	revealing	outspoken

8 Tick (✓) the correct answer. According to the text, why is punctuation important?

- **a** It allows readers to speed up and read faster. ______
- **b** It adds to the emotion of what is being read. ______
- **c** It provides guidelines on how to read text correctly. ______
- **d** It tells you when a sentence ends. ______

9 What have you learnt about Shakespeare that you didn't know before reading the essay?

____

____

____

____

____

____

____

Boost your reading skills

Understanding paragraph organisation

Paragraphs are the building blocks of an essay. A paragraph should **discuss** one idea in detail and **support** the development of an overall essay idea. Being able to read, understand and locate the different sections of a paragraph will assist your essay writing skills.

The basic paragraph consists of three parts: a **topic sentence**, **supporting details** and a **concluding sentence**.

An effective topic sentence expresses a paragraph's main idea and can help the reader more readily understand a paragraph's purpose. Generally, the topic sentence is the first sentence of a paragraph and subsequent ideas are used to support this main idea, also known as a **thesis**.

1 Read the following **paragraph ideas** and then choose a **topic sentence** for each one from the list.

Paragraph ideas

i William Shakespeare's work is considered an important landmark in the history of the English language.

ii There can be no doubt that Shakespeare was a master of the English language.

iii Shakespeare's modern influence is still seen clearly in many ways.

a He wrote with such flexibility of thought, word, rhythm, and sound that the work appears complex. However, it is not meaningless, even for new readers.

b For example, the success of Shakespeare's works helped assist the development of modern dramas and plays. He is also credited with being one of the first writers to use modern words in his plays and poems.

c The extraordinary writing skills with which Shakespeare created his truthful descriptions of life have not been matched since his death, nearly four hundred years ago.

Supporting details elaborate upon the topic sentence and help **support** or **prove** the main idea of the paragraph.

The following are common ways to provide supporting details:

- expert opinions
- facts and statistics
- examples
- definitions
- explanations
- quotations
- brief stories
- comparisons.

2 Look back at paragraphs 2, 3 and 4 and identify one or two ways those paragraphs have been **supported**.

Paragraph 2: ______________________________

____

Paragraph 3: ______________________________

____

Paragraph 4: ______________________________

____

Each paragraph should end with a **concluding statement** that ties together the paragraph ideas and emphasises the main idea one last time.

3 Read each of the possible **concluding statements** on an essay about Shakespeare and language. Tick (✓) the two best examples.

a Few modern writers have such skill to write in such a way that their words become common usage centuries later. ______

b Most people dream of experiencing love like Romeo and Juliet, which is why the most famous Shakespearean scenes is the balcony scene. ______

c William Shakespeare's genius, in part, lies with his ability to create new words that are in today's English language. ______

d His enormous effect on poetry is seen when considering how far his poetry and sonnets have influenced modern poets. ______

Work on words

Transition signals

Transition signals give a paragraph **cohesion**, **unity** and **organisation** because they guide the reader from one idea to another. They are used to **join sentences**, **idea groups** and **paragraphs** together. You need to take particular notice of them when reading essays and other formal texts, so that you become confident with using them when writing your own essays.

Compare the following two sentences:

> I sometimes find Shakespearean language difficult. I love watching his plays on the stage.
>
> I sometimes find Shakespearean language difficult. **Nevertheless,** I love watching his plays on the stage.

The relationship between the ideas in the sentences has changed through the use of the transition signal *nevertheless*.

1 The **transition signal** you choose will vary depending on your **purpose** for using it. The table below contains examples of different groups of transition signals. Label each of the groups with one purpose from the list. The first one has been done for you.

Purpose of the transition signal

- to contrast ideas
- to compare ideas
- to conclude ideas
- to order by time
- to add information
- to show the result of something.

Purpose of the transition signal	Examples of the transition signal
to add information	in addition, moreover, furthermore, besides, in fact, also
	after that, before that, then, at first, since, firstly, lastly, finally
	as a result, consequently, therefore, thus, hence
	in conclusion, in summary, finally
	on the other hand, in contrast, nevertheless
	similarly, also

2 Look at these sentences from the Shakespeare essay. Underline the **transition signal**, then using the list above write down the transition signal's **purpose**. Remember, the transition signal does not always occur at the beginning of a sentence.

a In addition, Shakespeare even took the liberty of inventing over one thousand frequently used words and expressions.

b In conclusion, despite Shakespeare's work being in constant use, he is not often given credit for his profound impact on the English language.

c Punctuation forces the reader to pause and slows down the pace of the text. Consequently, lines without punctuation naturally seem to gather speed and emotional purpose.

d Shakespeare's impact on the English language may never be repeated; however, we will always have the benefit of his insightful and powerful work.

e Conversely, it is not necessary to do this unless the punctuation, such as a full stop, specifically requires this to occur.

Spotlight on language

Formal or academic language

Reading and understanding the differences between **formal** language and **informal** conversational language that is used in everyday situations will help you understand academic texts. Formal language is a feature of written texts such as essays, business letters, reports, announcements and letters of complaint.

Choosing a more formal alternative when selecting a **verb** can add to the formality of a text.

For example:

Informal—The student **read** the newspaper to **find out** what was happening in the news.

Formal—The student **examined** the newspaper to **determine** the state of current affairs.

1 Replace the following underlined verbs with a more **formal verb** from the list. You may need to change the verb tense. The first one has been done for you.

assist advance determine establish increase eliminate

a The school had ___established___ a new system for ordering lunches.

b The student discovered ________ that they needed to work together in order to complete the project.

c My Shakespearean dictionary really helped ________ me to interpret the language.

d I've noticed a jump ________ in the number of students using the library.

e The teacher said that in order to improve ________ my rank I needed to study more.

f I would really like to get rid of ________ bad habits that are slowing me down.

Nominalisation

Nominalisation is one aspect of formal language used in written texts such as essays and reports. Nominalisation is usually when **verbs** are turned into **nouns**.

For example: *acceptance* (noun) from *accept* (verb).

When this happens, the **action** of the sentence becomes more important than the **person** who is completing the action.

Look at this example:

We argued with the government about the environmental issue (*argue* is a verb)

Our argument with the government was about environmental issues (*argument* is a noun)

Nominalisation also occurs when nouns are made from **adjectives** and **adverbs**.

For example: *difficulty* (noun) from *difficult* (adjective), *reality* from *real* (adjective) or *really* (adverb).

Understanding nominalisation when reading will help you when writing essays. It will help you create a **formal** and **academic tone**, to 'pack in' meanings to your sentences and to write in a general way about the topic rather than about specific experiences.

2 **Common suffixes** used in the nominalisation process are *tion*, *ment* and *al*. Add one of these to the following verbs in order to change them to nouns. The first one has been done for you.

- **a** frustrate frustration
- **b** argue ______
- **c** refuse ______
- **d** govern ______
- **e** propose ______
- **f** nominalise ______
- **g** advance ______
- **h** submit ______
- **i** inspire ______
- **j** introduce ______
- **k** promote ______
- **l** reflect ______

3 Underline the **nominalisations** in the sentences below. In the space below each example rewrite the sentence in **less formal**, everyday speech. Try to keep the complete sense of the sentence. The first one has been done for you.

- **a** No animal communication has the infinite capacity and complexity of human language.

  Animals cannot communicate in the infinite and complex ways that humans can through language.

- **b** Shakespeare was truly unique in his observation and mastery of our language.

- **c** Interpretation of Shakespearean language must be done with caution because of the changes over time in the meaning and usage of many words and phrases.

- **d** Considerable misunderstanding and confusion has arisen in relation to Shakespeare's early years and education.

- **e** Shakespeare's popularity and renown is not confined to the English speaking world.

Extend your skills

Research some further information about William Shakespeare's life and works. Record your findings here in a structured paragraph that uses **transition signals** to connect ideas and **nominalisation** to create a formal and academic tone.

UNIT TWELVE

Persuasive posters

Before you read

It is always easier to understand what you are reading if you have some **background knowledge** and **experience** of the topic. Activating this knowledge and experience helps you make connections between new and known information.

1 How much do you know about women during the Second World War? Mark the following statements True (T) or False (F).

- **a** Many women were actively involved as nurses and in other active service duties. ______
- **b** Women were actively recruited into jobs that had always been the domain of men. ______
- **c** Women were paid at lower rates than men and expected to 'step down' and return to home duties after the war. ______
- **d** Women were strongly encouraged to help the war effort by joining voluntary organisations. ______
- **e** Many women enjoyed participating in the workforce during war-time. ______

2 During times of war there are two main locations of importance—the war-front and the home-front. What do you think are the main activities that occur at each of these locations and by whom?

- **a** the war-front ____________________
- **b** the home-front ____________________

Rosie the Riveter and *Women*

Test your understanding

1 Looking at the title and picture of the first image, 'We can do it!', what do you think *it* could be?

____

____

____

2 Tick (✓) the correct answer. The character in image one became known as 'Rosie the Riveter'. Based on the image, who or what do you think a riveter is?

a an interesting and fascinating person ______
b a metal presser ______
c a seamstress ______
d a factory worker ______

3 What are your first impressions of Rosie?

____

____

____

4 Tick (✓) the correct answer. Taking note of the pictures and words in both images, what do you think is the main purpose of these images?

a to describe different women's jobs ______
b to persuade women to get involved ______
c to discuss women's war involvement ______
d to inform about historical events ______

5 Tick (✓) the correct answer. When Rosie says 'We can do it!', who do you think *we* means?

a riveters ______
b women involved in active service ______
c women at the home-front ______
d the whole of society ______

6 Tick (✓) the correct answer. What is Rosie doing with her arm?

a rolling up her sleeve ______
b making a rude gesture to the viewer ______
c she is about to punch someone ______
d flexing her muscles ______

7 Why do you think she is doing this?

____

____

____

8 Tick (✓) the correct answer. Image two states that 'There's work to be done'. Looking at the images, what kind of work does it refer to?

a physical work typically undertaken by men ______

b military service, such as nursing ______

c hospitality work, such as waitressing ______

d a, b and c ______

9 In Image 2, why do you think the word 'NOW' is printed in red and capitalised?

______

______

10 Tick (✓) the correct answer. What emotional response do you think the posters would create in women during war-time?

a fear of invasion by enemy countries ______

b excitement at the possibility of gaining employment ______

c empowerment and a sense of responsibility ______

d anger and aggression towards the enemy ______

Boost your reading skills

Reading visual texts

Persuasive posters are a form of communication aimed at influencing the attitude of the community toward some cause or position. It presents only one side of an argument and rarely tells the 'whole' truth of a situation.

During WWI and WWII on the home-front, these posters were used as an effective tool to persuade women to join the war effort. As there was a lack of employable males to complete jobs such as working in factories and construction, many women were enlisted through marketing to leave the domestic environment of the home and to fill the shoes of the men who had left to fight in the war. They were an effective persuasive tool as they created an **emotional response** in their **target audience** (the particular group of people the poster is aimed at). **Strong visual images** are carefully constructed to create an emotional response in the target audience.

Visual literacy is the ability to understand and interpret information presented in the form of an image. Visual literacy is based on the ideas that pictures can be 'read'. We can analyse an image for meaning by taking into account the body language and clothing of characters as well as the angle from which they are observed and the direction of their gaze.

- **Angle**—the angle from which objects are presented has an important effect on what the viewers see. The five basic angles are overhead, high angle, eye level, low angle and undershot. Angle is always described as being from the perspective of the viewer, not from the object's perspective.

1 Looking at image one ('Rosie the Riveter'), which **angle** are we positioned to view her from?

______

______

2 What is the effect of having her presented from this **angle**?

3 The **angle** used for image two is different. From which angle do we view the action?

4 What is the effect of this choice of **angle**?

> * **Body language** and **clothing** can communicate how figures are feeling and convey information about their personalities. They also have a significant influence on the tone of the text.

5 For 'Rosie the Riveter' circle the four best words that describe her **body language**.

masculine aggressive acquiescent essential macho destructive powerful

6 What **message** is being delivered to women of the time?

7 What **visual contrast** do you notice in the way Rosie is presented?

8 Identify four different activities undertaken by the characters in image two, 'Women'.

9 Why has the illustrator included this range of activity?

> * **Gaze**—where characters in texts are looking. They may be either looking directly at the viewer—this is called a '**demand**'—or they are looking elsewhere within the text—this is known as an '**offer**'. A demand is considered more challenging and aggressive than an offer, which may be more suggestive and less forceful.

10 Rosie is gazing straight at the viewer in a forceful way. What is she **demanding**?

11 The women in image two are looking elsewhere in the text and not at the viewer. What does their **gaze** suggest?

Work on words

Word associations

Making **word associations** is an effective way to help you form **connections** between words and to **develop** and **extend** your vocabulary. You start with a focus word such as *war*, which is a key concept of our topic, and brainstorm words that relate to this single focus.

For example: some words associated with war include *aggression, struggle, conflict, bloodshed, history, damage, danger, deadly, despot* and *uniform*.

1 What other words **associated** with *war* can you think of?

You can see that it is easy to quickly develop a long list of words associated with the topic. Using a **word map** can help you **organise** your words as well as make **connections** between words.

2 Expand the mind map by finding other appropriate words for the spaces.

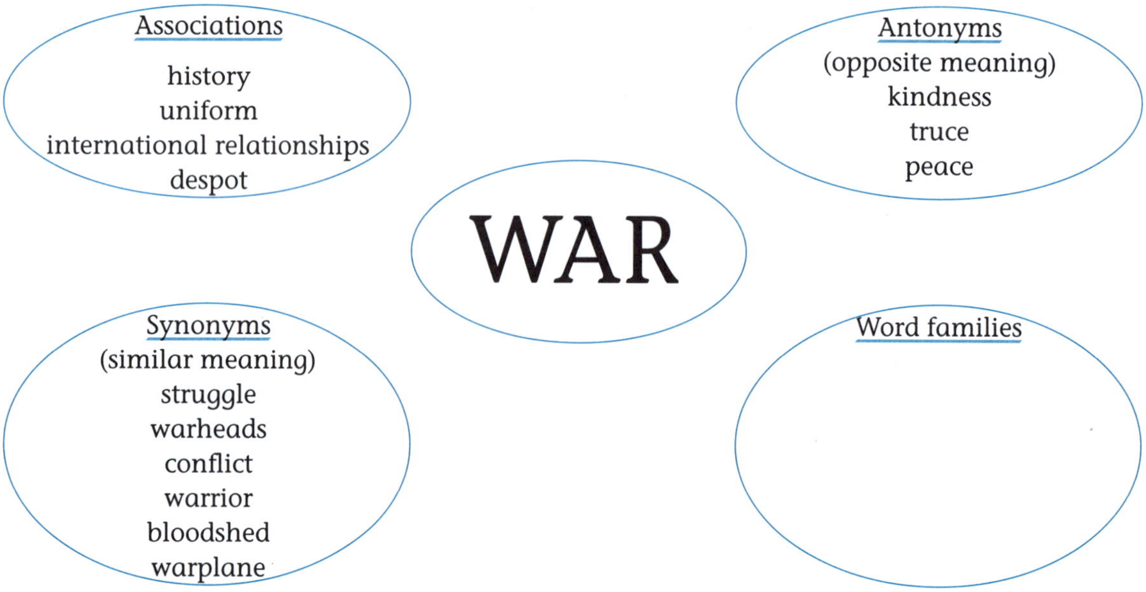

WAR

Associations
history
uniform
international relationships
despot

Antonyms
(opposite meaning)
kindness
truce
peace

Synonyms
(similar meaning)
struggle
warheads
conflict
warrior
bloodshed
warplane

Word families

Clines

A **cline** is a scale of language items that goes from one extreme to the other, such as from positive to negative, or from weak to strong.

Creating clines allows you to increase your sensitivity towards **subtle differences** between words, as well as **reinforce** your **understanding** of word meanings.

For example: infinitesimal—tiny—small—short—tall—big—huge—enormous—gigantic—humungous—titanic—immense

This example illustrates ideas about size, with the smallest examples on the left building up towards the largest on the right.

Some words in clines will be almost identical in meaning, but their use will be dependent on **context**.

For example: you would not use *humungous* in all situations.

3 Using the list of **synonyms** for war, plot them on the following **cline**, with the weakest examples on the left, increasing to the strongest examples on the right.

police action—battle—schism—conflict—skirmish—world war—falling-out—brawl—debate—civil war

4 Now try it with **descriptive words** associated with war, rating them from least to most dangerous.

deadly—brutal—dangerous—malicious—cold—violent—terrifying—bitter

Spotlight on language

Modality in persuasive texts

Modality is often an aspect of persuasive texts because the aim of these texts is to express a point of view and persuade the reader/viewer to share the same view. **Modality** expresses **degrees** of **probability**, **certainty** or **obligation**. It influences the **tone** of the text and allows the writer to **soften** or **intensify** the language to meet a particular purpose.

1 Use a **cline** again to plot these examples on a continuum from **low possibility** to **certainty**.

almost—always—rarely—never—always—occasionally—usually—sometimes

2 **Low modality** is a word or phrase that expresses uncertainty. **High modality**, on the other hand, expresses very certain ideas. Mark the following examples as having either high modality (HM) or low modality (LM).

a We need women to join the workforce immediately. ______

b With certainty, many women enjoyed participating in the workforce during war-time. ______

c Most women will probably return to domestic life after the war. ______

d There could be job opportunities for older women. ______

e Go and join the army now—your country needs you. ______

f I should join the war effort but I don't have time. ______

High modality used in persuasive texts has a **commanding effect**. The audience is influenced by the high level of certainty communicated by the text.

3 Change the following examples from persuasive posters so that they are expressed with **lower modality**. There are a number of ways in which this can be achieved. The first one has been done for you.

a We can do it! We might do it!

b There's work to be done and a war to be won … now!

____

c No water—no guns … don't waste it!

____

d We're in the army now—your aid is vital.

____

e We want you!

____

f I'm proud … my husband wants me to do my part!

____

4 In your own words, what do you think is the overall change in effect after modifying the examples above from **high** to **low modality**? Remember: the high modality effect is authoritative and commanding.

____

____

____

____

____

____

____

____

Extend your skills

The use of **persuasive texts** is a feature of our modern world. Everywhere you go you will encounter examples of persuasion: radio, television, brochures, advertisements and community announcements. War-time posters are often interpreted as being negative; however, some examples of persuasive posters are designed to help people's lives.

Create a community service poster that uses persuasive techniques to persuade the public that dropping rubbish, such as plastic and cigarette butts, is harmful for the community—and for waterways in particular. Use **modality** and **visual language** techniques to persuade people to dispose of their rubbish thoughtfully.

Answers

UNIT 1 SBS Reporters' blog

Before you read pages 2–3

1 Answers will vary.

2 Answers will vary. People will have different opinions on this topic and may feel a connection to people, places, or things. Some people may write qualities in this response (e.g. mateship, honesty, loyalty or compassion).

3 Answers will vary. Australia is generally considered more 'multicultural' since the 1980s. The notion of 'real' Australians being white and from an Anglo background is outdated and no longer represents our modern, vibrant and diverse population.

Test your understanding pages 4–5

1 c an SBS television presenter

2 a an inside look at the experiences of a television presenter

3 c social commentary

4 c to discuss what it means to be Australian

5 a culturally varied
b make english
c resulting in
d mixture
e a fixed idea

6 c named

7 b rejecting people based on perceived cultural differences

8 a what it really means to live as an Australian

9 Answers will vary. In the lead up to Australia Day, the author provides examples of his own experiences as an Australian from a multicultural background in order to promote harmony and acceptance.

Boost your reading skills pages 5–6

1 a Aussie, big deal, woggy, that's pretty Aussie
b (and the chance to get some publicity and attention for myself …)
c melting pot, throwing a shrimp on the BBQ

2 a I spent the first five years of my life speaking Portuguese …
b As we approach Australia Day …
c I was your typical Aussie kid growing up … That's pretty Aussie, (don't you think)

3 The personal pronoun *I* personalises the reporter's blog. It allows the reader to become involved in the writer's life and story and appreciate and perhaps empathise with their experiences.

We is an inclusive pronoun that has the effect of making the reader feel included and part of an experience.

The second person *you* or *your* works to include the reader in what they are reading. It makes the reader feel as if they are being personally addressed.

4 Answers will vary but may include:

Neither Ricardo nor his family really questioned his name change or made a commotion about it; it occurred on its own. Instead of being called Ricardo at school, he was known as Richard. The peculiarity was that he attended one of the most ethnically diverse Catholic primary schools in Wollongong, so the name change did not occur as a result of his cultural background or as an attempt to anglicise him.

Work on words pages 7–8

1
- **a** Busy as a bee.
- **b** On a wild goose chase.
- **c** The early bird catches the worm.
- **d** Good things come to those who wait.
- **e** A penny saved is a penny earned.
- **f** An apple a day keeps the doctor away.
- **g** Don't put all your eggs in one basket.
- **h** Wake up and smell the coffee.
- **i** Better late than never.
- **j** Raining cats and dogs.

2
- **a** Australia contains a variety of different nationalities all living together.
- **b** I consider myself to be a typical, archetypal Australian.
- **c** The name Richard was attached to me for 24 years.
- **d** The answers are clear, distinct and simple.
- **e** When he commenced/began/was launched into primary school, the nuns called him 'Richard'.
- **f** Neither I nor my family really questioned it or made a fuss/created a problem about it.

Spotlight on language pages 8–10

1
- **a** Great post. As far as stereotypes go, we're all immigrants, unless you're a full **blooded** Aboriginal. As far as I'm concerned, if you live here, you're an **A**ussie. Simple as that. Celebrate it in whatever takes **your** fancy, as long as it doesn't get ugly for others. That's REALLY 'un-**A**ustralian'. Happy Australia **D**ay to all at SBS. Whether we see/hear you or not you're all a bunch of champions in my book.
- **b** **T**hanks for your thoughts. **I** love to read stuff like this, so that **I** shouldn't have to define myself as '**A**sian **A**ustralian'. **A**ll the more power to the likes of you (us). **I** love having you as my hero and role model <3

2
- **b** sad: miserable, depressed, wretched
- **c** bad: wicked, corrupt, ruthless, unscrupulous
- **d** angry: annoyed, irritated, fuming
- **e** small: minor, trifling, insignificant
- **f** big: immense, vast, enormous

3 Answers will vary but may include:
- **a** I particularly liked your idea about racism and appearance because it reminded me not to judge people on their appearance.
- **b** I would like to compliment you on your blog. It made me feel interested when you mentioned your cultural experiences as I too have had similar things happen to me.

4 Answers will vary but may include:

Where do you see Australia heading in the future? Will attitudes towards people from other countries change and become more accepting? How did you feel when you were refused entry into the club?

Extend your skills page 11

Answers will vary. Some stylistic areas present in blog comments include the following:

- an informal style that is conversational
- personal language of opinion: *I think, I believe, I hope*
- present tense: *I am.*

You might like to respond to some of the ideas of the blog comment already posted.

Before you read pages 12–13

1 Alice Pung is not the author of the stories. The key words in the first 3 questions that indicate this are: **edit** (meaning that she has edited/overseen/revised the book, not written it herself), **selecting** (meaning that she had a selection/choice/assortment of stories to choose from) and **submission** (meaning that other people have submitted/proposed/suggested stories for her to approve and include in the selection.

2 *Black Inc. Books* is the publishing company responsible for publishing the memoir *Growing up Asian in Australia* that is edited by Alice Pung.

3 As the Q&A is published by the publishing company, the overall purposes of the Q&A will be to inform potential readers about its content as well as attract readers' interest and persuade them to buy it.

Test your understanding pages 13–15

1 **d** the editor of *Growing Up Asian in Australia*

2 **c** dealing with real events and people and based on truth

3 **c** deficiency

4 Answers will vary. *Diverse* here means 'varied and different interpretations' of the definition. *Inclusive* means a definition which is broad and which does not exclude certain groups'. She wanted to include stories which are a positive affirmation of Asian-Australian experiences and which do not divide individuals or groups of Asian-Australians.

5 Answers will vary.

6 **b** It turns people's expectations of how Asians live and behave upside down.

7 **d** there are no common themes as each story is unique and diverse

8 Answers will vary. Pung does this to show that Asian-Australians do not fit into any particular mould and are in fact all different, unique and diverse.

9 **a** a humorous thought and reflection on multicultural food in Australia

10 the anthology aims to focus on what makes us all human

11 **a** A model minority is a small group that contains ideal and desirable personality traits.

Boost your reading skills pages 15–16

1 **b** Although it rained a lot we still spent hours at the beach when we were kids.

c We loved to go away in the car during school holidays.

d After school I hope to continue study at university.

e He felt much better after realising other people felt the same way.

f The people who I grew up with are still my friends.

2 **a** Although this collection is titled *Growing up Asian in Australia,* I wanted to bring out the common humanity of our authors, so that any reader could pick up the book and be amused, amazed, moved and heartened.

b I concentrated on the period of 'growing up'—because that's the period when most of life's 'firsts' happen—and I also wanted the definition on Asian Australian to be as diverse and inclusive as possible.

c I was very happy about the incredible amount of interest received after calling for submissions.

d We also have quite a few stories about how different generations dealt with their parents and I only wish I had this amount of insight when I was growing up!

e Our younger contributors have a wonderful freshness of voice, but we were also especially honoured to receive stories from Asian- Australians from older generations, because they could reflect back on their growing-up years with the wisdom of experience.

f I wanted this anthology to encompass as much diverse insight as possible, so our authors come from every walk of life.

Work on words pages 16–17

1 **b** least **c** pore **d** current **e** currant **f** proceed **g** precede **h** averse **i** adverse

2 Answers will vary but may include:

a I need to adapt to my new environment quickly.

b She is adept with tools and will fix your shelf on the weekend.

3 **a** I need to ensure I get a new alarm clock before tomorrow.

b We need to insure our new house against fire and damage.

4 **a** I would like to compliment you on your lovely dress.

b That lemon sauce complements the fish so nicely.

5 **a** The strong effect of the coffee will have me up all night.

b I hope the wind and rain won't affect your holiday too much.

Spotlight on language pages 18–19

1 **b** It was embarrassing to be good at studies and I tried to hide my scholastic abilities as much as possible.

c I'd watch them intently: like an outsider, like a tourist.

d My attempts to blend in failed as soon as I opened my mouth.

e Now that I thought about it, everything up to that point in my life seemed so incredibly abnormal compared to everyone else I knew.

f To this day I am to some extent confused ... am I more Asian or Australian?

g If I couldn't express myself, who was my self?

2 Answers will vary but may include:

a I couldn't live without the internet or Facebook! How would I keep in touch with everything?

b I wish my mum and dad would talk to me more about stuff that's important to me.

c I wish people could understand what I'm thinking and feeling. I think they've forgotten what it's like to be young!

d I just felt like doing it, so I did, even though I knew it would get me into trouble

e I want to eat healthier as I know it's good for me and may help clear up my skin

Extend your skills page 19

1 and **2** Answers will vary.

Before you read pages 20–21

1 Answers will vary. You may trust that the information is reliable and 'true'. You may know that some people consider Wikipedia unreliable as it is not necessarily created by experts of the topic.

2 Answers will vary. You may use Wikipedia regularly as this option often pops up during Google searches when researching.

3 Answers will vary. Wikipedia can be a good source of research information; it is also known for providing up-to-date information on pop-culture subjects such as actors, musicians, films etc.

Test your understanding pages 21–22

1 **c** Oodgeroo Noonuccal

2 Oodgeroo Noonuccal was born with the name given by her parents (Kathleen Jean Mary Ruska). Kath Walker was her married name. When she grew older, she explored her indigenous heritage and adopted the indigenous name *Oodgeroo Noonuccal*. Being known also as 'Oodgeroo' suggests she is so well-known that her first name suffices to indicate her identity to many.

3 **b** information that helps you pronounce her name

4 **a** he was a political activist

5 **c** a hyperlink

6 **a** symbol

7 **c** She did not enjoy school because she was not permitted to write with her left hand.

8 Answers will vary. Historically, Aboriginal people had fewer rights and Oodgeroo experienced discrimination as an indigenous person. When war time came, many indigenous people contributed to the war effort and for a brief period were regarded as socially equal.

Boost your reading skills pages 22–24

1 Answers will vary. Having many general and unnecessary words will create a wide search result, whereas a narrower search will result in more efficient locating of ideas.

2 Answers will vary but may include:

What other poetry has Oodgeroo Noonuccal written?

a The key words are: poetry Oodgeroo Noonuccal

b Maybe words: written

c Words changed: written (created, authored)

d Unnecessary words: what, other

e Final search terms: ~ written Oodgeroo Noonuccal poetry

Work on words pages 24–25

1 b links—**image 6**
c podcast—**image 7**
d RSS—**image 4**
e wiki—**image 5**
f World Wide Web—**image 3**
g multimedia—**image 2**

2 Answers will vary.

Spotlight on language pages 25–27

1 All are correct, except f. Wikipedia is useful as a starting point for research and information, a place to locate background information on a topic, a place that will provide links or sources for further research. Due to the speed at which information can be updated on the internet, Wikipedia is often a likely location for late breaking news, information on new technology and information on popular culture.

2 Yes. The Oodgeroo Noonuccal Wikipedia article contains short titled sub-headings that move from general early life information to specific important features from her adulthood. The paragraphs are visually accessible, well-defined and separated.

3 Answers will vary but may include:

Aboriginal, Kabul, POW, book-keeping, short-hand, Harold-Holt. These words are all nouns and proper nouns that are hyperlinked to further information. 'Little' words such as the, an, in, it are never hyperlinked in Wikipedia pages.

4 Answers will depend on the individual. Readers may not know what 'Kabul' is or some of the references to war such as POW.

5 Answers will vary. Allowing access to the detail of the editing history is useful for looking at topics that are in a constant state of change.

Extend your skills page 27

Answers will vary.

UNIT 4 Gothic fiction

Before you read pages 28–29

1 Answers will vary. You may note Poe's talent, his struggle, his increasing drinking and his ultimate descent into mental illness.

2 Answers will vary. You may feel sympathy for Poe's hardships, intrigued by his life, or have a sense of Poe's life being very different from your own.

3 The word *grotesque* means surreal, weird, strange, bizarre, and fantastic. *Arabesque* is an ornamental design consisting of intertwined flowing lines, originally found in ancient Islamic art. On the basis of the meaning of these words, you might expect Poe's stories to be very unusual and complex fantasy stories.

Test your understanding pages 29–31

1 a P b P c P d U e P f U

2 Answers could include: Clouds hung oppressively low, Passing alone, Dreary tract, Within view of the melancholy house

3 d setting

4 a in a rural location

5 c especially

6 Answers will vary. The words *insufferable gloom* indicates the deep sense of unbearable depression and melancholy that the narrator experiences upon first viewing the house.

7 c that changing some details of the house would lessen its terrible effect

8

tarn	conquer, overpower, crush
sedge	provoking, pushing, stirring
lurid	a person loudly enjoying themselves
annihilate	lake, pond, body of water
reveller	garish, striking, vivid
goading	awe-inspiring, overwhelming
sublime	grass-like plant that grows in wet areas

9 melancholy, depressed, icy, unnerved, horrified

10 Answers will vary.

11 **a** 1800s

12 Answers will vary. The story is set during a time that is pre-cars as the narrator is on horse-back. There is no mention of 1900's technology and the author uses old-fashioned language.

13 Answers will vary.

Boost your reading skills page 32

1

Features of orientations	**A general example not from the Poe story)**	**Example from *The Fall of the House of Usher***
Physical-Emotional response	My heart pounded and my knees knocked. I couldn't breathe from fear.	I looked upon the scene before me … with an utter depression of soul. … nor could I grapple with the shadowy fancies that crowded upon me as I pondered.
Image of setting	The barren earth crumbled, dry and lifeless under my shoes.	**Clouds hung oppressively low, Bleak walls**
Image of character	His eyes stared vacantly from two dark-ringed sockets.	**I had been passing alone**
Questioning that challenges readers' thoughts	So, who do you think you are anyway, coming over like this, uninvited and unwanted?	**What was it that so unnerved me**

2 This vagueness adds an element of mystery to the story. The reader has a feeling of loneliness and of having been dropped in the middle of no-where. The reader might form an image in their mind's eye about the narrator. This image comes from the words he uses and the general impression of the scene.

Work on words pages 33–34

1 **b** curdled—**T** **c** secret—**M**
d suddenly, rushed—**U** **e** dread, fear—**T**

2

Words in the story	Examples
Words associated with horror	**dull, dark, soundless, oppressively, dreary, desolate, terrible, decayed, shadowy fancies, ghastly, melancholy, pervaded, torture, sublime, mystery, annihilate, precipitous, unruffled lustre, goading, lurid**
Words that show the narrator's fear	**alone, insufferable gloom, iciness, sinking, sickening, dreariness of thought, unnerved, grapple, shudder**
Words used to describe the house	**bleak, vacant, eye-like windows, rank sedges, black, lurid tarn**

3 The author's use of vivid description places the reader at the scene with the narrator. We cannot help but experience his discomfort and terror at first beholding the house of Usher.

Spotlight on language pages 34–36

1 The narrator is uncertain about the source of his discomfort as he regards the house—*What was it—I paused to think—what was it that so unnerved me in the contemplation of the House of Usher?*

2 The accumulation (build-up) of information about the house makes the reader nervous and suspenseful towards the house, as does the use of personification. This is when Poe assigns the house human qualities ... *vacant eye-like windows.*

3 The pacing is slow. There is not much action during the story's orientation. Complex sentences and punctuation such as dashes add to the sense of the narrator's internal dialogue and psychological discomfort.

4 The narrator has a strong and negative reaction to the house. The reader wonders what will happen when he enters the house and if its effect on him will worsen.

5 The narrator hints at a *mystery all insoluble* (unsolvable). As he gets closer to the house he ... *gazed down—but with a shudder even more thrilling than before,* which indicates that even stranger and more scary events may occur.

6 The repetition creates an effect of accumulation, whereby the building up and increasing of sinister features about the house has an effect on the reader.

7 Answers will vary but may include:

Feature of gothic stories	What it symbolises
wailing winds	**emotional turbulence, pain, sorrow**
strong rain	**tears, loneliness, isolation, fear of extreme natural phenomenon**
ruins of buildings	**desolation, isolation, decaying mind or body**
baying of distant wolves	**danger, treacherous nature, threat, approaching danger**
absence of sound	**supernatural, anxiety, tension**
approaching footsteps	**anticipation, urgency**
thunder and lightning	**emotional turbulence, scientific experiments**

Extend your skills pages 37

1 A musical instrument is something that can be 'played'. People's emotions and relationships can also be 'played' upon, or manipulated.

2 These lines describe a heart so alone that it is poised and ready for touch, and so sensitive that it will *resound*—reverberate, echo or vibrate—the moment it is.

3 Loneliness, isolation, unrequited love, misunderstandings, secrecy, disturbance, relationships.

UNIT 5 Travel writing

Before you read pages 38–39

1 Answers may vary. Bush medicine involves using natural resources such as trees, shrubs, berries and herbs to heal and soothe physical ailments. It mainly derives from indigenous people's use.

2 Answers will vary. The adjective *rough* indicates that this travel guide may focus on less-expensive, unusual or off-the-beaten-track travel experiences and advice.

Test your understanding pages 39–40

1 **d** Australia's landscape contains remedies and cures as well as dangers.

2 **d** explore

3 **b** discovering medicinal plants

4 **d** the Tea Tree plant.

5 **b** It is useful in a variety of situations.

6 **c** sound, sight and feel

7 The track is not established and therefore unclear—'While you concentrate on the barely distinguishable path'.

8 **a** Despite support, it's difficult to stand on the slippery slope.

9 **d**, **a**, **b** and **c**

10
- **a** sharp
- **b** sculptured
- **c** added
- **d** coated
- **e** fitting
- **f** incline
- **g** spontaneous

Boost your reading skills pages 41–43

1 Methodology means procedure, order, approach. The article will contain information on how bush medicine is made and also what is involved in bush medicine.

2
- **a** Generally, bush medicine is made from plant materials
- **b** In general, there are two types of accepted causes of illness in aboriginal tribes—natural, and supernatural.
- **c** Aboriginal remedies varied between clans in different parts of the country.
- **d** Traditions in southern and eastern Australia have largely been lost

3 Answers will vary.

4 Answers will vary.

5
- **a** In a country where a small spider can kill you, it's reassuring to know Mother Nature has a softer side.

  These ideas contrast with one another. They show the extreme nature of the Australian country. The paragraph may focus on Australia's 'softer side', meaning less dangerous features of nature.
- **b** One of the first things you are struck by as you descend into the chiseled gorges of the park is the smell—an astringent mix of eucalyptus and tea tree, a result of the oils evaporating from these plants which also gives the air its blue haze.

  The paragraph may focus on specific Australian plants; the eucalypt and tea-tree, and their function and effect on the natural environment.
- **c** Descending further, the hum of cicadas gets louder and the air becomes humid as you enter the moss- and lichen-encrusted cloud forest.

6 This is a physical description of the experience of being within the Australian bush. The present tense use of 'descending' gives the reader the feeling of experiencing the event as well. The paragraph may continue with a description of the physical experience of being in that environment.

Repetition of proper nouns such as Australia and Aborigine create a clear focus for the article's ideas. Proper nouns such as New South Wales, Blue Mountains National Park and Wentworth Falls provide specific locations. Historical information is provided through nouns such as WWII and colonial. Other nouns such as moss, bush pears and vine set this article more specifically in a bush location.

Work on words pages 43–44

1
- **a** a quick shower
- **b** fast food
- **c** high ceiling

2 **a** strong **b** big **c** small **d** big
e take **f** to **g** heavy

3 **c** make **d** make **e** do **f** do
g do **h** make **i** make **j** make

4 Answers will vary but may include:

- **b** wrong side
- **c** down side
- **d** each side
- **e** off side
- **f** weaker side
- **g** bright side
- **h** safe side

Spotlight on language pages 44–46

1 **a** Descending further, the hum of cicadas gets louder and the air becomes humid as you enter the moss- and lichen-encrusted cloud forest.

Senses stimulated: Auditory, tactile, visual

b While you concentrate on the barely distinguishable path, your eagle-eyed guide will point out everything from bush pears, an ancient Aboriginal snack, to the aptly named headache vine, once crushed and rubbed directly into the skin to treat migraines.

Senses stimulated: Visual and tactile

c As the air grows warmer and your spirits start to flag, your ears will welcome the hiss of the nearby Wentworth Falls, signaling both the hike's end point and the prospect of an invigorating swim.

Senses stimulated: Tactile, auditory

d One of the first things you are struck by as you descend into the chiseled gorges of the park is the smell—an astringent mix of eucalyptus and tea tree, a result of the oils evaporating from these plants which also gives the air its blue haze.

Senses stimulated: olfactory, visual

e Walking ancient hunting tracks used by indigenous peoples, far from the car parks and crowded viewpoints, you will discover a different side to this wonderful national park.

Senses stimulated: Tactile

2 Answers will vary but may include:

- **a** Low grey clouds, pregnant with water, hung ominously in the darkened sky like ghostly galleons.
- **b** The sound of small children shrieking in the water pierced my skull like daggers.
- **c** The storm smelled of dank seaweed that wafted up from the water's edge.
- **d** The swimming pool water embraced my skin in an explosion of cool.
- **e** The humidity filled my mouth with the taste of warm salty fog.

Extend your skills page 47

Answers will vary but may include:

Bondi, Australia's most famous beach is a smiling pale stretch of soft sand and azure waves. Attracting travellers, surfers and families, it's one of Sydney's favourite spots for people-watching and café cruising.

The beach is a popular spot for surfing lessons, volleyball, yoga and events at the Pavilion that overlooks the beach with art deco authority. Lifeguards patrol the often hazardous waves, so it's important to swim between the red and yellow flags.

Bondi is overlooked by a long line of shops, restaurants and cafes for post-beach dining and relaxation. Scenic coastal walks lead from Bondi to the local beaches of Clovelly and Bronte.

If you have children then you will love the kiddie paddling pool at the beach's north end. A community-created mosaic overlooks the pool and delights children with colourful and whimsical depictions of ocean-life. I paddled there and was enchanted to see small children splashing noisily, crowing with delight and sharing buckets and spades.

Both spectacular and friendly, Bondi is a must-visit on a trip through Sydney.

UNIT 6 Shakespeare

Before you read pages 48–49

1 Shakespeare's play *Othello* is a tragedy because of dark and negative themes that occupy it. Key words from the summary that indicate this include: deadly, jealous, evil, malicious, unfaithful, and suspicious.

2 **a** ambitious—having or showing a strong desire and determination

b malicious—full of, characterized by, or showing malice; malevolent; spiteful

c plot—a secret plan or scheme to accomplish some purpose, especially a hostile, unlawful, or evil purpose

d jealous—feeling resentment against someone because of that person's rivalry, success, or advantages

Test your understanding pages 49–50

1 **c** the act of speaking one's thoughts aloud when by oneself or regardless of any hearers

2

Othello	the speaker, a character with evil intentions
Desdemona	a character who Iago will use to undermine Desdemona's strong reputation
Iago	Othello's wife and the person Iago will manipulate in order to seek revenge against Othello
Cassio	'the Moor', in other words a person who comes from North Africa

3 **b** Othello loves her so deeply that she may easily influence him.

4 **b** ironic. Iago is clearly not 'honest'.

5 **d** Cassio

6 **d** to help Cassio gain favour with her husband

7 Answers will vary. Iago is attempting to destroy Othello indirectly, through his wife Desdemona. He will achieve this by undermining Desdemona's good name and by placing doubt in Othello's mind.

8 **d** That she repeals him for her body's lust

9 Answers will vary. Complex themes of jealousy, rejection and revenge are universal due to their ability to relate and remain relevant to modern audiences. Throughout the play, issues regarding sexism and racism come to light by examining character interactions. The play offers value as a text due to its ability to examine human nature and its flaws.

Boost your reading skills pages 50–52

1

a	Anon, good nurse! Speak!	exclamation of disgust
b	Thou art dead; no physician's art can save you.	right now
c	Dost thou know the time?	before
d	We must leave ere daybreak.	are
e	I fain would bake my teacher a cake if I could get an A.	does or do
f	You cheated? Fie upon it! (upon you?)	gladly

2

a	Listen to the bird	hath
b	Come here young lad	hark
c	He has a horse	whence
d	You are a villain	hither
e	Your name is more hateful than your face	art
f	Return to where you came	whyfore
g	Why dost thou leave?	thy

3 *False* means to be fake and dishonest. *As hell* is used to effect here to mean 'very' and creates a strong contrast with *heaven* that works to intensify the insult.

4 A toad is considered ugly and venomous—a toad is regarded generally as something repulsive. A *toad* is known figuratively as a disgusting person.

5 This insult provides many strong visual images regarding the physical appearance of the person being insulted—who is described as being physically large and repellent, as well as diseased, an over-eater and *vain*, meaning narcissistic, self-important and egotistic.

Work on words pages 52–53

1 **b** frugal **c** impartial **d** perusal **e** lapse **f** baseless **g** sanctimonious

2 Answers will vary.

3
- **a** foregone conclusion
- **b** In his heart of hearts
- **c** the green eyed monster
- **d** At one fell swoop
- **e** pomp and circumstance

Spotlight on language pages 54–55

1
- b villain/honest
- **c** Divinity/hell
- **d** honest fool
- **e** malicious bravery
- **f** Excellent wretch

2
- **a** *Pestilence* is a metaphor for the 'poison' or lies that Iago is giving Othello. It is information that will hurt someone. Iago is lying about Desdemona's relationship with Cassio and 'poisoning' Othello's relationship with her.
- **b** *Pitch* is a noun or 'thing' meaning 'black'. It is used here as a metaphor for blacken, or darken. Iago plans to undermine Desdemona's 'white' and honest reputation and make it appear she is being unfaithful to Othello.
- **c** A net is dangerous as it is a tool for tricking and trapping people. Here, the *net* Iago refers to is the complicated and suspicious relationships that Iago is creating. The *net* Iago is making is a trap that will entangle and ensnare Othello.

Extend your skills page 55

Answers will vary. A sample response is provided:

1 Act 2, scene 3 of *Othello* is significant as it reveals the true motives of the character of Iago. Iago is one of the most notorious and mysterious villains of all time. He spends all of his time plotting against Othello and Desdemona, eventually convincing Othello that his wife has been cheating, despite the fact that Desdemona has been completely faithful.

2 The extract explores complex themes of jealousy and revenge. Iago speaks from malevolence: 'And what's he then that says I play the villain, when this advice is free I give, and honest?' He has now refined his plan and outlines the diabolical details: Cassio will plead with Desdemona, who will plead with Othello. Iago will tell Othello that Desdemona desires Cassio. "I'll pour this pestilence into his ear" Iago will whisper poisonous words into Othello's ear, killing Othello from the inside by filling his mind with unbearable jealousy.

3 In Iago's soliloquy, Shakespeare employs metaphors that create strong images in the reader's mind of Iago's evil intentions. 'Pestilence' is a metaphor for the 'poison' or lies that Iago is giving Othello. He is lying about Desdemona's relationship with Cassio and 'poisoning' Othello's relationship with her. 'Pitch' is a metaphor for blacken, or darken. Iago plans to undermine Desdemona's 'white' and honest reputation and make it appear she is being unfaithful to Othello.

4 Iago reveals his true character during Act 2, scene 3 of *Othello*. Through his character, Shakespeare explores notions of villainy and evil and reveals ideas about human weakness.

UNIT 7 Political speech

Before you read pages 56–57

1 The Stolen Generations (also known as Stolen children) were the children of Australian Aboriginal and Torres Strait Islander descent who were removed from their families by the Australian Federal and State government agencies and church missions. The removals occurred in the period between approximately 1909 and 1969, although in some places children were still being taken until the 1970s.

2 To be indigenous means to have: strong links to a territory, distinct social, economic or political systems, and distinct language, culture and beliefs.

3 The government had not previously apologised to indigenous people about the effect of past policies and decisions. The act of saying sorry, of apologising, is very powerful and can assist people to heal and move on with their lives.

Test your understanding pages 57–59

1 **b** he apologises completely, with no exceptions

2 **b**, **c** and **d**

3 **d** ripped apart, pain, suffering, humiliation

4 **a** Kevin Rudd's words can't change the past, but he hopes they will inspire a new beginning.

5 **d** a desire to resolve past problems and move forward

6 **b** '… unless the great symbolism of reconciliation is accompanied by an even greater substance, it is little more than a clanging gong'.

7 **d**, **a** and **c**

8 Answers will vary. *Closing the gap* means to reduce and lessen differences between indigenous and non-indigenous Australians in areas such as length of life, educational outcomes and employment opportunities.

9 Answers will vary. The apology focuses Australian society on the future, on ways to move forward as well as ways to improve experiences for indigenous communities.

Boost your reading skills pages 59–61

1 passionate—ardent, fervent
practical—concrete, real-world
reconciliation—reunion
clanging gong—meaningless event
indignity—humiliation
degradation—deprivation
embodied—exemplified, demonstrated
powerful—potent, influential
accepted—acknowledged, recognised
resolve—decide, agree
inadequate—insufficient, lacking
wrongs—crimes, injuries, injustices

2

Noun	Adjective
symbol	symbolic
apology	**apologetic**
degradation	**degradative**
pain	**painful**
parliament	**parliamentary**
humiliation	**humiliated**
substance	**substantial**

3 **b** The government apologises for **parliamentary** decisions that resulted in hurt and **painful** suffering.

c The laws resulted in indignity, humiliation and had **degradative** consequences.

d Reconciliation will only be **symbolic** unless it is accompanied by something **substantial**.

4 Answers will vary but may include:
The government's **admission of guilt**, however *inadequate*, is aimed at righting *past* **mistakes**. It is also aimed at building a *respectful* **relationship** between Indigenous and non-Indigenous Australians—a *deferential* **connection** based on a *real* **esteem** rather than a *poorly-disguised* **disrespect**.

Work on words pages 61–62

1 **b** vitality **c** alienate **d** stalemate
e pseudonym **f** gamut

2 **b** benevolent **c** congenial **d** propagate
e inferior **f** noxious

3 **b** **take away**—reduce, lessen, diminish

c **crippling effect**—devastation, desolation, ruin

d **past wrongs**—mistakes, violations, infringements

e **building a bridge**—linking, connecting, joining, amalgamating, uniting, fusing

f **a clanging gong**—pointless, futile, meaningless, ineffectual

Spotlight on language pages 63–64

1 **a** discomfort **b** discourtesy
c disagreeable **d** weakening
e enthusiastic

2 Kevin Rudd's repetition of two key phrases 'I am sorry' and 'We apologise' focuses his audience on the purpose of his speech. He personalises the apology through the use of first person 'I', and reinforces this by widening his apology to include the government and parliament 'we'. There is strong pathos and depth of emotion created.

3 **a** A bridge is a metaphor for a relationship, or connection. Kevin Rudd hopes to build a strong relationship between all Australians.

b The *bridge* or relationship should be strong and based on positive and respectful feelings and emotions, rather than focussing on past negatives—"... **a bridge** based on a real respect rather than a thinly veiled contempt"

c *Crossing the bridge* is a metaphor for the challenges or hurdles indigenous and non-indigenous people face in attempting to strengthen their relationship.

Extend your skills page 65

1 Answers will vary.

UNIT 8 Autobiography

Before you read pages 66–67

1 *Speaking from the grave* means that you are dead by the time people read your words.

2 **b** because he can speak honestly and without obstruction

3 **c** the past

Test your understanding pages 67–69

1 **c** present—present—past

2 **d** is fearful talking about what he really thinks and feels

3 **a** insignificant
c minor
f small

4 **a** metaphor

5 **b** working, in action, thinking

6 **d** to explain that we are more our thoughts and feelings, rather than our actions and words

7 **b** his thoughts

8 **d** biographies rarely express a person's inner thoughts

9 **b** he wanted to protect his children's financial future and success

10 **c** his generosity did not result in the family's happiness or good fortune

11 **a** reflective and informative

Boost your reading skills pages 69–70

1 **a** first person
b third-person limited
c third-person omniscient
d first person or third-person limited

2 **a** first person
b third-person omniscient
c third-person omniscient
d first person
e third-person omniscient

3 Twain uses **two** main narrative points of views—first person and third person **omniscient**. He uses first person when talking about his real life experiences. First person narrative **personalises** the experience and provides the 'voice' of the narrator. It also focuses the reader on the writer's life and **experiences**.
Twain shifts to third person omniscient point of view when talking about the wider experience of life and writing. In doing so, Twain creates a sense of a **shared** experience and is able to speak for 'all' people.

Work on words pages 70–71

1 Answers could include: autograph, automatic, automation, autocracy, autopilot, autopsy, autonomy

2

cryptic	put into code/expressed in code
encrypted	a hidden vault
cryptology	the text part of a message that is in coded form
crypt	deliberately mysterious with a hidden meaning
crypto text	the study of encoding and decoding plain messages

3

Definitions	Prefix examples
a wheel, circle	democracy, epidemic, demographic
b through, across	hydraulics, hydrant, hydrophobia
c people	monoplane, monotone
d race, nation	cyclone, cycle, bicycle
e blood	pneumatic, pneumonia
f water	geography, geometry
g one, alone	pyromaniac, pyrotechnics
h air, breath	diameter, dialogue
i fire	haemorrhage, anaemia
j earth	ethnic, ethnology

Spotlight on language pages 71–73

1 a personification b simile
c metaphor d personification
e metaphor f hyperbole

2 "All the world's a stage, and all the men and women merely players;
They have their exits and their entrances; And one man in his time plays many parts."

3 a A man's acts and words are compared to a visible thin crust. This is a metaphor for how people appear to the outside world—they show only a thin veneer of their whole selves.

b His thoughts and feelings are represented as the Earth's core or parts beneath the 'crust'

4 a a man's personality is more complex than it appears on the outside, or 'crust'

5 Answers could include: restless, anxious, thoughtful, agitated, thinking, moving, active, alert, working

Extend your skills pages 73–75

Answers will vary.

UNIT 9 Environmental article

Before you read pages 76–77

1 b mistakes made in computer disposal. The article's heading and subheading touches on all topics listed in the question, but will have the key theme of recycling and computer disposal

2 Answers will vary.

3 Answers will vary. Some people may just throw them in the bin, keep them in a drawer, or dispose of them through a company or recycling program.

4 Answers will vary. Correct recycling of these items is important as they pose a risk to the environment when not correctly disposed of.

Test your understanding pages 77–78

1 c electronic waste

2 c jam packed, crowded

3 d in the future

4 It is cheaper to just buy a complete new unit rather than buying smaller parts and upgrading sections of a computer.

5

a actively discarded (paragraph 1)	basic components
b teeming landfill (introduction)	cathode ray tube
c crude materials (paragraph 1)	deliberately thrown away
d CRT (paragraph 1)	restoring or overhauling units
e refurbishing old systems (paragraph 3)	basic or simple resources
f constituent elements (paragraph 4)	overflowing tip or rubbish dump

6 **c** dismantle safely then recycle

7 This means that some countries may highly value old computer systems and make excellent use of them.

8 **b** to inform and persuade

9 Answers will vary. Some people may be surprised by the importance of recycling e-waste or be unaware of correct practices surrounding it.

10 Answers will vary. The article is highly relevant to an Australian audience. As a western country, issues relating to the environment and computer waste and recycling affect Australia as much as countries like America. As a wealthy country, we should also be aware of our potential to donate technology to those in need.

Boost your reading skills pages 79–80

1 e-waste, computer, recycled, environment

2 Yes, these words are the article's key words as these main themes are developed and further explored throughout the rest of the article

3 The heading and sub-heading are written in bold. These provide clues to the ideas of the article and act as a summary of the article's main themes and ideas.

4 ... 40 million units, ... nearly three quarters of the computers sold in the US are gathering dust

5 CRTs alone contain lead, cadmium, mercury, beryllium and other hazardous materials.

6 Some of the printed circuit boards contain precious metals such as silver, gold, and platinum.

7 ... constituent elements like metal, glass and plastic

8 Answers will vary. Most *good* and accessible websites are organised using the scannable text features.

Work on words pages 80–81

1 **b** manner **c** number
d degree **e** time **f** time

2 **b** manner (how)
c manner (how)
d time (when)
e degree
f manner (how)
g degree

3 **b** really **c** properly **d** good
e quickly **f** badly **g** than

Spotlight on language pages 81–82

1 **b** My mother and I both have the same phone.

c Many parts of the telecommunications system were destroyed by the storm

d The unused classroom near the library is going to be redeveloped into a computer room.

e Standing on the roof at the top of the house was a large aerial and satellite dish.

f During holidays we often text about lunch.

g Lying on the beach with a good kindle book is my favourite thing to do.

2 **b** ~~The only limits~~ to this are ~~the limits of the human imagination~~.

c Creative thinking is all that is needed to ~~expand the future possibilities for computer recycling~~.

d This is ~~landfill waiting to happen~~

e Some of the printed circuit boards contain ~~precious metals such as silver, gold and platinum~~.

f They also contain ~~base metals like iron and copper~~.

Extend your skills page 83

Answers will vary but may include:

What is e-waste?
The term 'e-waste' includes all old electrical appliances either in a state of disorder or simply outdated. This includes everything from fridges and microwaves to mobile phones and computers. The correct disposal of ewaste is of essential importance to being able to achieve a sustainable future.

E-Recycle is Australia's leading e-waste collection and recycling service. We're dedicated to collecting as much electronic waste from landfill and export as possible. For too long, metals such as mercury and lead found in computers and other ewaste have been buried in landfill, leaving the toxins to leach into the ground and waterways.

The E-Recycle service is professional, quick and trustworthy. We collect your e-waste from your door and deliver it to the appropriate recycling facilities where it will be recycled for future use.

Before you read page 84

1 Answers will vary. Some people may think that the older style poem contains old-fashioned words or ideas. The poem will be about a past time in Australian history and may be associated with the bush.

2 Answers will vary.

Test your understanding pages 85–86

1 c an invented character—a literary critic

2 b original.

3 c it stopped suddenly and interrupted the beat of the poem.

4 a a rhythm of syllables that creates an internal beat to the poem as it is read

5 The critic is scratching his head while he is thinking about the poem and critiquing it. The poet relies on the critic's knowledge and wisdom as guidance.

7 a an aside by the character.

8 b to work long and hard at night

9 c an idea with a certain charm, that has something memorable about it.

10 a the beat, sound and ideas in the poem.

11 b humorous—despite all the persona's work, the poem has lost its originality.

12 a reflective and self-critical.

Boost your reading skills pages 87–88

Title—the word *my* indicates that the poem will be told from a personal perspective. Someone who is 'literary' is bookish, scholarly, academic and so the poem may contain themes relating to literature.

Point of view—the poem is being told from the perspective of an unnamed character, who has written a poem and is having it assessed and critiqued by a *literary friend*.

Theme—the poem shows the difficulties in writing poetry that is interesting, original and well-structured. It also shows that it is not always beneficial to seek another's advice during the creative process and you may have to change your original ideas quite dramatically.

Poet's purpose—the poet wrote the poem to highlight the process of creativity. He explores ideas around accepting criticism from others, and that you really need to remove your ego from the process of writing, or you may be disappointed.

How does the poem sound? The poem 'sounds' quite quick and it has a fast pace. This is due to examples of repetition 'so' and 'it' as well as its strong and catchy rhyming scheme. The reader is forced to slow down at points—particularly during the 'asides'; (I believe in taking time) as these interrupt the flow of the poem's rhythm.

Word pictures—the poet uses occasional images that create a picture in the reader's mind.
(e.g. 'scratching surplus wisdom from his head' and 'burnt the midnight taper')

Work on words pages 88–89

1 **Formal**: praised, surplus, wisdom, suggested, succeed, conceited, solemn
Informal: good, thing, straighten'd, bad, midnight taper, a ring about it, jingle, horrors

2

a	Than e'er it ran before	unemployed, unoccupied, lazy
b	For the commonwealth of idlers	ever
c	'Twas Mulga Bill, from Eaglehawk, that caught the cycling craze	remote from major populations
d	That would tide him o'er the morrow	ought to
e	Where the scrubs and plains are wide	It was
f	And the time had come, as the shearer knew, to carry his swag Out Back	low, thick bush
g	magpie up in the scrub, and yer oughter be able to catch it.	over

Spotlight on language pages 89–91

1 a puff/enough

2 a wood, stood
b cloud, shroud
c night, white
d time, prime
e bells, foretells
f breath, dizzy, death, easy
g dreary, weary, lore, napping, tapping, rapping, door, door, more

3 a ABAB
b ABAB BCBC CDCD EE

4 AABB CCDD EEFF GGHH

5 In many **simple** poems, the final words in successive lines often rhyme. You may have noticed this in simple poems like nursery rhymes. Typically, this style of rhyming can become **predictable** and fairly boring, and poets who choose to rhyme usually add greater **variation**. Henry Lawson's use of a simple rhyme scheme works well, however. He has **deliberately** chosen this simple rhyming scheme as it enhances the light-hearted and **humorous** effect of the poem.

Extend your skills page 91

Answers will vary.

UNIT 11

Essays

Before you read pages 92–93

1 English, language, transition, history, Shakespeare.

2 The essay will be about the English language and Shakespeare. It will be about how the language has changed over time.

3 b Shakespeare's influence on our language

4 With Shakespeare's creation of commonly used expressions, his formation of new words, and his use of punctuation, he was able to affect language in a way that was unprecedented.

Test your understanding pages 93–95

1 change, development, progression

2 b to inform and persuade about Shakespeare's great influence

3 c Shakespeare affected and influenced the English language.

4 c shaping

5 b Lines with no punctuation increase the pace and feeling of what is being read.

6 d Reading into the next line without pausing creates a sense of natural speech.

7 a not ever done before
b opportunity
c exposed
d clear
e thoughtful
f well-expressed

8 c It provides guidelines for how to read text correctly.

9 Answers will vary

Boost your reading skills pages 95–96

1 **a** **ii** There can be no doubt that Shakespeare was a master of the English language.

b **iii** Shakespeare's modern influence is still seen clearly in many ways.

c **i** William Shakespeare's work is considered an important landmark in the history of the English language.

2 **a** Paragraph 2: examples

b Paragraph 3: additional details and examples

c Paragraph 4: explanation

3 **a** Few modern writers have such skill to write in such a way that their words become common usage centuries later.

c William Shakespeare's genius, in part, lies with his ability to create new words that are in today's English language.

Work on words pages 96–97

1

Transition signal purpose	Transition signal examples
to add information	In addition, moreover, furthermore, besides, in fact, also
to order by time	after that, before that, then, at first, since, firstly, lastly, finally
to show the result of something	as a result, consequently, therefore, thus, hence
to conclude ideas	in conclusion, in summary, finally
to contrast ideas	On the other hand, in contrast, nevertheless
to compare ideas	similarly, also

2 **a** In addition—to add information

b In conclusion—to conclude ideas

c Consequently—to show the result of something

d however—to contrast ideas

e Conversely—to contrast ideas

Spotlight on language pages 98–99

1 **b** determined **c** assisted **d** increase
e advance **f** eliminate

2 **a** frustration **b** argument **c** refusal
d government **e** proposal
f nominalisation **g** advancement
h submission **i** inspiration
j introduction **k** promotion **l** reflection

3 **b** Shakespeare was truly unique in his observation and mastery of our language.
Shakespeare was unique in the way he was able to observe language and become a master in how it was used.

c Interpretation of Shakespearean language must be done with caution because of the changes over time in the meaning and usage of many words and phrases.
We must be cautious when we interpret Shakespearean language because what words mean and how they are used has changed over time.

d Considerable misunderstanding and confusion has arisen in relation to Shakespeare's early years and education.
Many people misunderstand and are confused about Shakespeare's early years and where and how he was educated.

e Shakespeare's popularity and renown is not confined to the English speaking world.
Shakespeare is popular and well known in non-English speaking countries of the world as well as English speaking countries.

Extend your skills page 100

Answers will vary.

UNIT 12 Persuasive posters

Before you read pages 101–102

1 All the statements are TRUE of women during war-time.

2 **a** A war front is the region where a battle is being or has been fought. It's the line along which opposing armies face one another.

b Home front is the informal term for the civilian (non-combatant) populace of the nation at war as an active support system of their military. Combat soldiers depend on home front civilian support services such as the factories that build material to support the war front.

Test your understanding pages 102–103

1 It's not clear what *it* is as there is very little information given in the text. The audience is being encouraged to take action, to contribute, to achieve something with and for people with a common purpose.

2 **b** a metal presser

3 Answers will vary. She is looking towards the viewer in a direct way. She is making a strong, masculine looking physical gesture with her arm. She looks capable and no-nonsense.

4 **b** to persuade women to get involved

5 **c** women at the home-front

6 **d** flexing her muscles

7 Rosie is showing that she is just as strong and capable as the men who are away on the war front. The two world wars, especially the second, were important in showing the feasibility of women holding traditionally male jobs.

8 **a**, **b** and **c**

9 This communicates the urgency with which the government requires capable women to step into roles traditionally dominated by men.

10 **c** empowerment and a sense of responsibility

Boost your reading skills pages 104–106

1 We view Rosie from an eye-level angle.

2 The eye-level angle is effective as it creates a sense of reality and naturalness. The viewer and Rosie are presented as being equals.

3 We view the women's activity from a high angle (we look 'down' on them).

4 Although high angles can be used to create feelings of vulnerability, in this case it just allows us to observe the busy activity of the women in the image.

5 masculine, aggressive, macho, powerful

6 Women are being persuaded to join the war effort on the home front. This is achieved by making them feel empowered and capable of taking on 'men's' work.

7 Rosie wears a masculine military-type outfit that is contrasted by her feminine 'house-wife' head scarf.

8 Answers could include: waitressing, riveting, mechanic, nursing, bread-making, fixing, building, administration.

9 The illustrator is showing the wide range of activities women are capable of undertaking in order to contribute to the war effort. There should be something there that everyone could do.

10 Rosie is demanding that women join her in work that will support the war-effort.

11 The women's gazes indicate how busy they are. They are employed in a wide-range of activities that are supporting the war-effort and are intent and focussed on their work.

Work on words pages 106–107

1 Answers will vary but may include: aggressor, aircraft, alliance, ambush, battle, bunker, chopper, civilian, chaos, disaster, endurance, explode, forces, hospitalise, impact, infantry, jets, liberate, militant, prison, rebel, retaliation, survival, unit, violence

2 Answers will vary but may include:
Associations: aircraft, bunker, helicopter, hospitalise, liberate, survival
Antonyms: accord, harmony, peace, surrender, cease-fire, friendship
Synonyms: battle, bloodshed, combat, conflict, hostility, struggle contention, enmity, strife
Word families: Warfare, warden, war power, warmonger, wartime, warhorse

3 debate—falling-out—schism—conflict—skirmish—police action—brawl—battle—civil war—world war

4 cold—bitter—dangerous—malicious—violent—brutal—terrifying—deadly

Spotlight on language page 106

1 never—rarely—sometimes—occasionally—usually—almost always—always

2
- **a** HM
- **b** HM
- **c** LM
- **d** LM
- **e** HM
- **f** LM

3
- **b** There could be work to be done and there might be a war to be won … soon
- **c** Some water—some guns … could be wasted.
- **d** We're in the army now—your aid could be vital.
- **e** We might need you!
- **f** I could be proud … my husband might want me to do my part.

4 The change in modality drastically reduces the power and effect of the command. The message becomes less forceful, less urgent, and as a result less important.

Extend your skills page 109

Answers will vary.

Notes